HIGH PRAISE FOR
ONE DOOR CLOSES,
ANOTHER DOOR OPENS

"READ THIS REMARKABLE BOOK! Its stories, insight, and wisdom will help you overcome daily obstacles and will provide you with the determination, courage, and confidence to face the darkest moments in your life."

> —Wess Roberts, author of
> *Victory Secrets of Attila the Hun*

"An inspiring and easy-to-read collection of advice and anecdotes guaranteed to give a boost to anyone's spirits."

> —Barbara De Angelis, Ph.D.

"Pine won't give you a road map to success, but he will motivate you to draw your own, and also to be more aware of positive signs along the bleaker parts of the highway."

> —*The Port Washington Sentinel* (New York)

"CONSOLATION, GUIDANCE, COUNSEL AND INSPIRATION."

> —Martin Seligman, author of
> *Learned Optimism*

"A WINNER!"

> —*Port Chester Guide* (New York)

Please turn the page for more extraordinary acclaim . . .

D1051252

QUANTITY SALES

Most Dell books are available at special quantity discounts when purchased in bulk by corporations, organizations, or groups. Special imprints, messages, and excerpts can be produced to meet your needs. For more information, write to: Dell Publishing, 1540 Broadway, New York, NY 10036. Attention: Director, Diversified Sales.

INDIVIDUAL SALES

Are there any Dell books you want but cannot find in your local stores? If so, you can order them directly from us. You can get any Dell book currently in print. For a complete up-to-date listing of our books and information on how to order, write to: Dell Readers Service, Box DR, 1540 Broadway, New York, NY 10036.

ONE DOOR CLOSES, ANOTHER DOOR OPENS

Turning Your Setbacks into Comebacks

ARTHUR PINE

with Julie Houston

A Dell Trade Paperback

To my mother, "Granny Annie," as she was lovingly nicknamed by my children, David and Richard. Her calm disposition and optimistic attitude had such a great influence on my life. She is missed, as is my father.

Acknowledgments

Very special credit and thanks go to the following contributors to *One Door Closes, Another Door Opens,*
whose stories for this book are quoted verbatim. That
they so generously took the time out from their busy
schedules to share their wisdom and thoughts is appreciated beyond words:

Mary Kay Ash, Wally Amos, Milton Berle, David
Brown, George Burns, Carol Burnett, Sammy Cahn,
Kathy Cronkite, Walter Cronkite, Hal David, Phyllis
Diller, Katherine Dunn, Dr. Wayne Dyer, Gordon Edel-
stein, Leonore Fleischer, William Fromm, Larry Gelbart,
Harold Gershowitz, Skip Gladstone, Andrea Richman
Golden, Red Holzman, Ted Isaac, Tommy John, Sally
John, Martin Katahn, Ph.D, Melvyn I. Kinder, Ph.D.,

George Lang, Michael Levine, Christine McGuire, Ross McElwee, Diane Medved, Michael Medved, Robert Merrill, Sharon Mesmer, Ann Miller, Paul Nathan, Michael Newbrand, Jim Nicolson, James Patterson, Pat Riley, Wess Roberts, Dorothy Sarnoff, Edgar Scherick, Melville Shavelson, Dinah Shore, Hilde Serlin, Eve Silverman, Jack Smith, Liz Smith, Dan Sullivan, Rabbi Joseph Telushkin, Susan Weiner, Kathy Wood, and Henny Youngman.

I must also acknowledge with gratitude the outspoken candor of the following people whose stories, as covered in the press and media (and in some instances, through my own personal involvement), offer outstanding examples included in this book of what *One Door Closes, Another Door Opens* is all about:

Jeffrey Archer, Adrien Arpel, Kevin Costner, Greer Garson, Larry Holmes, Elton John, Michael Jordan, Mervyn LeRoy, Joan Rivers, Frank Sinatra, Margaret Thatcher, Edward Villella, Leslie Wexner, and Katarina Witt.

To all of these fine people, including the many others from all walks of life whose anecdotes are woven into the following pages, we offer sincere thanks. And for special advice and bits of wisdom that helped mold this book, appreciation goes to John Lampl, director of public affairs, British Airways, USA; Leonard Wurzel, Irwin and Linda Young, Lori Andiman, and many others.

And, of course, special love and thanks to all of the members of the Pine family, without whom I would not be the happy person I am—my wife, Harriette, sons David and Richard, their wives, Dale and Nancy, and our grandchildren Ross, Alec, Adam, and Gideon. How lucky can one person be!!!!!!

And, how can I forget my publisher-editor, Leslie Schnur, one of the most talented and nicest people in the publishing world—a real mensch.

Last but far, far from least, my coauthor Julie Houston, who did so much to put this book into shape and whose contributions are much appreciated.

Contents

Introduction

One door closes, another door opens. A negative becomes a positive. *Setbacks don't just happen, they happen for a purpose.* These are words to live by today more than ever. Each day we hear of things coming to an end. Businesses failing, people losing jobs, divorce rates skyrocketing, families falling apart, cities falling apart, political systems collapsing—doors are slamming at every turn, *and yet we still see people coming through with flying colors.*

A door closing should be thought of as a source of new strength, not as a failure. It should bring out the best in you. Those who are optimistic and able to fight off adversity use the wisdom of "One door closes, another door opens" as incentive to move ahead. Those who fall over and play dead remain losers throughout life.

Attitudes *can* change. The setback that leaves one person lying flat and immobilized galvanizes another person into action. You *can* change your attitude. If you have a pessimistic outlook on the future you *must* learn how to change it, if you are ever going to find that new and more satisfying beginning.

One door closes, another door opens. It's all about action. When something ends—a job, a relationship, one's good health—you just don't stand by and wait for something good to happen. You can't depend on luck or anybody else to pull you out of the situation. You must use your own efforts to push a new door open, *kick* it open if you have to, using that setback as an inspiration to move ahead and make a new beginning for yourself.

Something comes to an end, it knocks you down. We all get knocked down in life. Get back up and analyze the situation. Think of how you can change it for the better—make another door open; if need be, *create* a new one. Use this book as a source of ideas and inspiration. The following stories of one door closing, another door opening, prove beyond doubt that there are many, many ways to make this happen.

ARTHUR PINE

ONE DOOR CLOSES, ANOTHER DOOR OPENS

1

SO A DOOR CLOSES . . .
SO WHAT?

> *"What is defeat? Nothing but education;*
> *nothing but the first step to something better."*
> WENDELL PHILLIPS (1811–1884),
> *American orator and reformer*

A door closes.

It's not the end of the world.

Forces out of your control may have brought an opportunity to an end, but even then, it can lead you to something better.

A FIRING IS NOT SUCH A BAD THING.

Liz Smith credits the start of her career as a columnist to such circumstances; today she's the number-one syndicated show-business columnist and a major television personality:

I owe my current career as a successful syndicated gossip columnist to the Eisenhower recession. In other words, it was being fired after five years as a producer at NBC that set me onto another path. I thought I only wanted to work in "show business," but the necessity to find a job led my friend, the agent Gloria Safier, to recommend me to Igor Cassini. He was then writing the Cholly Knicker-bocker society column for the Hearst newspapers and needed an assistant. I went to work for Cassini and learned column-writing from the ground up. That lasted five years, and then I became a successful free-lance writer. In 1974 Mike O'Neill of the New York Daily News *urged me to come to work and write a gossip column for him. We spent two years backing and forth-ing, and in 1976 I did join the* News *and the rest is history. It wouldn't have happened without a recession in the fifties.*

Nobody relishes being fired from a job. But no matter what situation you are in, *you will land on your feet again* if you have complete confidence in yourself and your abilities.

BEING OUT OF WORK CAN WORK TO YOUR ADVANTAGE.

As Phyllis Diller found out, it can even launch a career:

I was flying along great guns on my own, booking myself into those wonderful discovery clubs such as the Purple Onion in San Francisco and the Hungry i; Mr. Kelly's in Chicago; the Blue Angel and the Bon Soir in New York. Then along came the "Big Important Agency" with the big guns and they booked me into places where I shouldn't have been, for a lot more money, but for total failure. One such place was the Fontainebleau Hotel in Miami Beach, at its peak when they were playing top entertainment—Frank Sinatra and his ilk. They booked me there and after my first show the manager fired me.

I came back to New York where I was based . . . based being a polite term for living in a fleabag hotel where people who were "on-the-way-ups" or "on-the-way-downs" stayed for sixty dollars a month.

My defeat positively paralyzed my big important agency. They thought, My God, we've picked a loser. However, my being fired, so shattering at the time, turned out to be a really important break because The Tonight Show's Jack Paar had just discovered me and liked me a lot. He believed in me.

"Out of work," in New York, and available for that great NBC show whenever Jack wanted me—this was the absolute basis of my rapid rise to fame. Jack used me on the show so often, and each show we did was such a hit, they all later became reruns and the exposure was tremendous.

There is no doubt I owe my success to a disastrous firing and Jack Paar's friendly exposure.

PLANNING YOUR NEXT SUCCESS

Making plans for your future success is a valuable exercise. The more control you have over a closing door, the better chance you have of making a positive experience come out of it:

Analyze the source of your unhappiness before you plan your next move.

Don't close a door on a job or relationship that appears to make you miserable when you could have made it better.

Before a couple announces they are breaking up, they would be wise to ask themselves: Do we really need to break up? Some couples are really perfectly suited for each other. They may split or divorce, marry someone, and then split up again. More frequently than not, couples who were perfectly compatible will break up and never find replacements as well suited to each as their mate.

Proceed slowly, but do proceed.

Some people sit back and say, "Boy, look at him or her. I'd love to be doing that sort of thing—run my own company, write a novel—but I just can't do that." With that attitude, believe me, nothing will happen. Give yourself a chance.

**If changing your situation
seems too overwhelming a
challenge, think of short-term
goals at first.**

The mountain climber doesn't go right to the
top. Sometimes he only goes a quarter of the
way up, and comes down. Next time he goes a
little farther, all the while finding the right
place to put his foot and his climbing equipment. It takes a lot of thinking to be that
mountain climber whose goal is to reach the
top; it takes just as much thinking to close a
door on yourself and climb up to something
better.

Closing doors in stages applies to personal
situations as well, such as ending a marriage or
relationship.

**Look ahead, think, and plan
for what you want to
accomplish, not just now, but
in the years ahead.**

Consider all possibilities—good times, bad
times. Analyze the situation, thinking ahead,
and act in a way that shows you know what
you're doing. Many people hasten toward a

career or toward retirement without a plan, but that can be a mistake.

Make up your mind what is important to you; what comes first and how to find a balance between job, family, your outside interests, or whatever it may be.

Determine your assets and skills and how you can apply them in other areas.

Consider working for yourself or starting your own business.

Owning one's own business means working hard, long hours, and gambling on financial investment. However, if you are an independent thinker and thrive on excitement, you may be well suited to be your own boss. Do your research; seek out advice. Lay your groundwork carefully. Attend business seminars; read everything you can get your hands on, including books, periodicals, and articles about entrepreneurship and starting a business. You need solid knowledge and expertise in the area you wish to pursue; confidence that you are in the right business at the right time.

TAKE THAT CLOSED DOOR AS A SIGN THAT FATE HAS OTHER PLANS FOR YOU.

This is what Robert Merrill, the great Metropolitan Opera baritone, discovered at the start of his career when he desperately needed a job. His brilliant career in opera never could have happened if he'd gotten the job he wanted!

In 1943 I auditioned for the number-one night spot in New York at the time, a club on Fifty-seventh Street called the Martinique. They needed someone to do the production number and they were paying a salary of $150 a week, an enormous amount of money at that time.

It was one of my first auditions, and I really needed a job. The owner liked operatic voices for the show and when I sang, he loved it and wanted to engage me right away, but the director who staged the shows had reservations. "You've got a good voice," he told me, "but I've decided to hire someone else, a fellow named Dick Haymes."

That was the closed door, and I felt just terrible. However, the following year I auditioned for the Metropolitan Opera, and a year after that I made my debut in La Traviata. If I had gotten that job at the Martinique, the door to the Metropolitan Opera never would have opened.

There's an interesting side point to this story as well. For Dick Haymes that job at the Martinique was the door

7

opening on his career. Nobody knew of him, it was his first appearance, and from there he went on to become a Hollywood star.

UNEXPECTED ROADS ARE WAITING TO BE TRAVELED.

Your original hopes and aspirations for a career may suddenly end, but who knows, that devastating closed door may lead you to another that opens onto an exciting new path in life.

Michael Medved's wife, Diane Medved, who is a psychologist and author of *The Case Against Divorce,* offers her own inspiring example of how talent can be applied to many different situations and careers:

> *Many years ago when I was finishing college, I trained to be a teacher. It was during the great teacher glut in California, but I thought I was well placed in the competition. I had done two assignments student-teaching at one of the first alternative schools in the state, and when a teaching post opened up there, despite the fact that there were 250 applicants for it including four other student teachers who had practiced there, I was convinced the job was mine because I wanted it more than any other teaching position in the world.*

After days of many interviews with administration and students, the candidates were narrowed down to two applicants—I was one of them. Now I knew I would get it for sure: I had gotten that far.

Except I didn't get it. I lost it. It was just awful and I felt as if my life were coming to an end. I had succeeded with most everything I'd gone out for in life, how could I not get this job? What was I going to do?

Well, I returned to school without my teaching plans and pursued my degree in psychology. That, in turn, brought me to my present career as a psychologist and a writer, which turned out to be absolutely perfect for me. I know now that I probably wouldn't have lasted as a teacher, but I am thrilled to be a psychologist and to combine that with writing books.

I once failed a teaching exam.

When I was a sophomore at City College in New York, I decided I would go out for a teacher's degree so that I could teach business subjects in the New York City high-school system. Teaching provided great security, good pay, and a ten-week paid vacation. To pursue my objective I had to take a challenging three-part examination (on a par with the one given to college graduates becoming teachers) that was given to sophomores, qualifying them for further course work toward the teacher's degree. I passed the first two parts of the exam—written English and mathematics—but I failed the third part, oral English. My diction did not come up to teaching standards, and on that basis I did not qualify to proceed toward a teaching degree. All my plans for the future went out the window.

When I got the news that I had not passed the test, I went into my bedroom and cried. I felt my world had come to an end. However, when I recovered from the shock of failure, I went back to school with a vengeance. I would use everything at my disposal to get ahead and do the very best I could do. I kept going with the course work I had been doing and specialized in marketing, advertising, and business administration. I increased my involvement in school activities. I wrote plays for the college performances. I graduated with a good deal more confidence and a wider range of experiences than I would have had if I'd pursued teaching. I could have quit college and gone out for a job that would have helped support our household, but my parents and I realized that a college education would serve me well in life, and it did. Being turned down for my major proved to be the best thing that ever happened to me. Instead of becoming a teacher, I ended up in the public-relations field and from there, eventually, I became a literary agent—more successful and satisfied with my work than I would ever have been with teaching.

When a door closes, do not panic. Take your time and think through your situation. Just wait and see—something great will come of it if you don't let it get you down.

Kevin Costner was thirty years old and the father of two daughters before his career took off. Even then it was due to a door closing—his part in *The Big Chill* ended up on the cutting-room floor.

For him that was fine. He says, "I knew when I was cast in *The Big Chill* I had lodged myself in that position where I wanted to be—in the company of good actors and a good director."

So a door closes . . . so what?

2

QUICK TURNAROUNDS

The moment when a door closes can feel like the end of the world, but it would be foolish to let it get you down, to give up hope.

Let the examples in this chapter be an inspiration in showing the speed with which "quirks of fate" can sometimes take the event out of one's hands—and the agony.

I BELIEVE IN ME—THAT'S WHAT YOU'VE GOT TO SAY TO YOURSELF.

In the days when she was first in New York, struggling to launch a career in the theater, Carol Burnett had her own experience of one door closing and another one quickly opening.

When she was called to audition for a revival of Rodgers and Hart's *Babes in Arms,* scheduled to open on Broadway in the fall of 1959, it looked as if her dream of having a lead part in a Broadway show was coming true. She had imagined that the legendary Broadway playwright and director George Abbott would be her first director, but in reality she would be more than satisfied just to be on Broadway, which was the prime reason she had come to New York.

The Broadway audition came—and went. "I knew I'd lost the part the minute I opened my mouth to read," Carol said. "I was awful."

Returning to her apartment where her sister Chrissy was hoping to hear good news, Carol described what had happened and burst into tears. Her sister gave her a hug and cheered Carol up with those very words my mother used to say to encourage me in such situations—"One door closes, another one opens."

In the kitchen preparing dinner, Carol was laughing again when the phone rang. It was a call for another audition—this time for a lead in the musical version of Hans Christian Andersen's "The Princess and the Pea" entitled *Once Upon a Mattress,* with George Abbott directing.

Carol got that lead part she had dreamed about, and of Mr. Abbott she says, "He was everything I dreamed he would be; under his magical guidance our modest little musical was one of the surprise hits of the season."

One door closed, another door quickly opened for Carol Burnett, and it can for you too. *Hope is the greatest remedy of all.*

Carol had the talent, the dream, and obviously had made the contacts, otherwise that wonderful telephone call giving her a big break in her career would not have come in. *Stick to your dreams. Do everything you can to realize them. The rest will take care of itself.*

YOU CAN'T SUCCEED EVERY TIME.

Playwright Larry Gelbart's experience with two Broadway shows in 1989 taught him his own special lesson about the quick-change acts of life. Larry Gelbart is coauthor of the Tony Award–winning stage musical *A Funny Thing Happened on the Way to the Forum;* developed and coproduced the television series *M*A*S*H,* and wrote the screenplays for *Oh, God!* and *Tootsie. City of Angels* was another Tony Award winner for best musical.

> *My play,* Mastergate, *closed on December 10, 1989. Rather prematurely, I thought, but then, doesn't every author think that? The following day, December 11, my musical* City of Angels *opened.*
> *On the night of the tenth, I was terribly saddened*

about one show folding and then, within twenty-four hours, I had the assurance that because of the critical reaction to City of Angels, *something new and exciting was just beginning. It was a joyful feeling, but one that was tempered by the sorrow of the night before.*

I was sixty-one years old in 1989, and unexpectedly here was a new experience coming my way that taught me 1) you're never too old to learn, and 2) hopefully, you'll have a little time ahead to practice whatever you learned from the experience. Having so many emotions compressed into such a time period was a good lesson in not letting myself get too "up" or too "down" about anything, because those highs and lows are just part of the game.

A DOOR COULD OPEN WHEN YOU NEED IT THE MOST.

When that happened for Michael Levine, former Drug Enforcement Agency group supervisor and international undercover agent, the situation seemed hopeless:

I was living alone on a government salary in a little apartment in New York, going through a divorce and recovering from a bad injury—during a drug raid I went out a window and ended up with three herniated disks, an impact fracture, and a shattered right knee. I was counting on the advance I would get from the sale of my book, Deep Cover, *to pay for the legal services in con-*

nection with a government lawsuit, and then, after months of waiting, I found out that the literary agent I was using hadn't sent the manuscript to one publisher. The door was closed in every direction. I was under investigation, going through a divorce, injured, totally broke, and no longer had any hope of publishing my manuscript. One more call to another agency. Arthur and Richard Pine read my manuscript, liked it, and in two months Deep Cover *was sold. It became a best-seller and I went on to a three-book deal, and a movie deal sold. Things worked out better than anything I could have imagined.*

LIFE IS FULL OF SURPRISES.

Sometimes a momentous change of plans unexpectedly alters circumstances, quickly turning disappointment into rare opportunity. Walter Cronkite experienced one such twist of fate when he was a young correspondent in Europe during World War II, just before the Allied invasion.

With D day approaching in England, I was disappointed with my assignment from the United Press ... disappointed, although somewhat flattered. I would not be going to France with the invasion troops but instead had been chosen to remain in London to help write the lead stories when the invasion story broke, a prestigious if somewhat less exciting assignment.

However, in the hours before the landing, I was awakened by an Eighth Air Force public-relations officer. A

17

last-minute change of plans would throw the bomb power of one B-17 Flying Fortress group at a particularly dangerous part of the Normandy coast.

One reporter would be permitted to go along, and my name had been drawn.

The officer said that I would have the first look at the landing and still be back in London before the D-day flash hit the wires. Provided my plane got back, of course.

Unfortunately, our flight back was delayed by bad weather and I got back a little late, but I still had the story of a great look at the Allied armada and the first fighting on the beaches of France.

Katarina Witt, the figure-skating champion from East Germany and gold medalist in the 1984 and 1988 Olympic Games, is an example of how, when history changes its course, impossible dreams suddenly come true for individuals who more than deserve them.

Down came the Berlin Wall, and up went Katarina's career:

A totally new world opened to me. I had a lot of possibilities after the Olympics, but I wasn't able to do them. It was like being in a box, knocking on the walls, screaming, "Please let me out!" Now I have so many possibilities. It's all so new, so wonderful. People come to me and ask me what I want to do.

Opportunities come along whether you're ready for them or not. They either happen, or you make them happen.

New doors will open—often quicker than expected.

Find ways to to keep your spirits up until that telephone rings, the letter of acceptance arrives, that new opportunity comes knocking at your door: Put a smile on your face—listen to oldies on the radio; look at old photos. Distract yourself with a positive project—rearrange the furniture in a room. Get outside. Window-shop, walk the dog, buy an ice cream cone, fly a kite, play games with a child, take a ride in the country.

3

DON'T GIVE UP!

"To be defeated and yet not surrender, that is victory."
JOZEF PILSUDSKI (1867–1935),
Polish national hero and freedom fighter

*"Victories that are easy are cheap. Those only are worth
having which come as the result of hard fighting."*
HENRY WARD BEECHER (1813–1887),
American clergyman

*"An enterprise, when fairly once begun,
Should not be left till all that ought is won."*
WILLIAM SHAKESPEARE (1564–1616)

When a door closes on something you fervently believe in or an opportunity you hate to lose, don't just walk away from it. Step back, look the situation over, and ask yourself this key question: *Is the door really closed?*

If there is a chance in a million that you can do something, *anything,* to keep what you want from ending, it is worth a try. Pry the door open or, if need be, wedge your foot in that door and keep it open.

WHERE THERE IS A WILL, THERE IS A WAY.

World-renowned speech consultant and author Dorothy Sarnoff describes the unusual measures she took to keep her singing career alive after doctors told her she would never sing again. Her story involves bad luck losing her first job after graduating from college:

I was just weeks away from starting my first job as the female understudy at the St. Louis Municipal Opera when I got a cold and laryngitis. Foolishly, I kept up with rehearsals and on top of the laryngitis, I lost my voice. I kept quiet, hoping I would be well again when I got to St. Louis, but I was wrong. My voice still wasn't right but I had no choice other than going ahead as scheduled. I stood onstage in front of a full audience in a play with Vincent Price, I opened my mouth, and nothing came out. Nothing.

There went my first job—and off I went to meet with the top throat specialist in the country. "I don't think you'll ever sing again," he said; "you'll talk, but I doubt you'll ever sing."

I was petrified. This was potentially a career-ending diagnosis for any vocalist. The doctor wanted to operate on my vocal cords, but one of my favorite sopranos at the Metropolitan Opera had had such an operation and her voice had never been the same. I had one other option besides surgery: to keep totally silent and give time a chance to heal my vocal cords. This is what I did. I remained totally silent for four and a half months, never speaking a word.

At the end of that time I was allowed to whisper ten words; soon after that, to speak ten words. The overtones were like big bells ringing in a tower, an unforgettable sound.

Six weeks after my recovery—six months after my nightmare of standing onstage without a voice—I became a finalist in the Metropolitan Opera auditions in New York, something that never would have happened if I'd been working in St. Louis. From there I became a leading soprano of the New York City Opera, starred in thirteen operas, performed with Gertrude Lawrence in The King and I, *worked at all the nightclubs, and appeared five times on* The Ed Sullivan Show.

Keeping the door open on one career, Dorothy Sarnoff inadvertently opened another one as well—as a world-renowned speech consultant. "When I lost my voice," she explains, "I vowed to learn everything about voice there was to learn so that what happened to me would never happen to anybody I knew. In the process I learned how to change the way people speak, to lower high voices, change resonance, and so forth, and that's how a whole second career started for me."

How many times have you seen a figure skater fall down and yet win the contest? A prizefighter get knocked down twice in a fight and yet come back to victory? A student start out with a grade C in the first marking period, and end the term with a B-plus or an A? When a good lawyer who believes firmly in a client's case loses that first round in court, how often does he or she use that defeat as a source of energy—to go on and try the case in a second, third, and even fourth court if possible? How many times is an "expert opinion" proven wrong?

KICKING CLOSED DOORS OPEN

If you spot a glimmer of hope behind a door that you hate to see close:

Take immediate action.

Give it all you've got to keep the opportunity alive. Wage an all-out campaign for kicking the door back open.

Put up a fight for what you want.

When Frank Sinatra lost his voice midway in his career, he could have just given up and faded away, but he would not let that door close. He had too much drive. When he felt his voice was ready he opened at the Copacabana in New York, which was the number one nightclub in America at the time. That performance was the beginning of a tremendous comeback that included an Academy Award for acting, record sales in the millions, and Frank Sinatra's solid place as one of the greatest entertainers in show business.

> ### Don't wait for a reply, force a reply.
>
> Don't worry that your persistence may seem bothersome; keep it up until you're told it is bothersome! Most people don't see it that way at all—tenacity is proof you really care about something. Take that extra step to seek out oral or written confirmation of where you stand, no matter what the bureaucracy, job, or situation you are dealing with. If you don't like the response, try to go past the bureaucracy to make personal contact.
>
> ### Mobilize the support of others to help you win.
>
> Move quickly to muster your allies. Show you have others on your side, and you will be taken seriously.

NEVER TAKE NO FOR AN ANSWER.

Skip Gladstone, a business administrator in a New York City law firm, kept up his job search—and proved "the experts" wrong:

The events on Wall Street in October 1987 had a major impact on the financial services company where I was employed. By 1989 the company had to downsize tremendously, and as part of the downsizing my position was eliminated. I went into outplacement counseling and determined that with my heavy administrative background, I should pursue work as an administrator in a law firm. However, I found out very quickly that law firms only wanted people who had worked in law firms.

Despite a great deal of rejection I did not give up. I did a tremendous amount of networking. I did a major mailing to all the law firms in New York City, but to no avail. Finally, I got one positive response—not a specific job offer but encouragement from an administrator in a law firm. My experience with rejection had paralleled his. He told me to keep going and eventually a law firm would recognize my background and potential. It turned out he was right. Before I knew it, I had landed an administrative job in a law firm—just what I wanted.

A REVERSAL ISN'T ALWAYS THE END OF THE ROAD, IT MAY JUST BE A DETOUR.

When a door closes on something you don't want to end, you've got to do what one of the great pitchers in baseball history, Tommy John, did when he suffered his arm injury—fight back!

My injury occurred during a night game in 1974, playing for the Los Angeles Dodgers. I was having the best season a baseball player could hope for—I was the leading pitcher in the National League; it looked as if I was going to win twenty games for the first time in my life and that the team was going on to the World Series. All the things that a small boy dreams about were happening to me and then suddenly, on one pitch, boom, it was all gone.

I'd ruptured a ligament—the elbow injury a pitcher fears most because surgery almost always means the end of a career. The procedure I needed had never been done before on a major-league pitcher, but I knew if I ever wanted to play again, I had no choice but to go ahead with it.

On September 25, 1974, Dr. Frank Jobe did the operation, and recovery was a long shot. I asked the doctors, "Do I have any chance of pitching again?" "About one out of a hundred" was their answer, but they were more candid with my wife, Sally: "Your job is to try to encourage Tommy to think of what he's going to do," they said to her, "because his pitching career is probably over."

One Sunday in church, with my arm in a cast and a beautiful baby girl who had been born two days after my surgery, we were sitting there, and the sermon was about Abraham and his wife, Sarah, who was well into her seventies before being blessed by the Lord and becoming pregnant with their first child.

As our minister read the story from the Bible, he looked up and said, "You know, with God, nothing is impossible." He was looking right at me when he said it, and I looked up at him and he kind of smiled, and I just marked it down in my Bible—there was what I needed to hear.

Sixteen weeks later, when the cast came off, my fingers had atrophied so much, my wife said my hand looked like a chicken claw. The arm had shriveled down to nothing—it looked as if it belonged to a ninety-year-old man. To hold anything I had to bend my fingers into place. Cutting meat, opening a door, was impossible. When Sally rubbed my skin with baby oil, it would all peel off in her hand.

When it came time for rehab, I spent hours and hours at the stadium. At the ballpark the trainers put me through a grueling series of exercises to strengthen the muscles.

Recovery progressed by inches. One day I remember coming home from the ballpark with my hands behind my back and telling Sally I had a surprise for her. She thought I was playing a joke on her, that it was a dead lizard or something, but then I stretched my left hand out from behind my back very slowly and bent the little finger to meet the thumb. We hugged each other and jumped up and down, shouting with joy; it was the first time I could move my fingers and it was as if I had gotten a bonus for a hundred thousand dollars. It was a sign that those muscles were finally coming back.

When I wasn't working with the trainers, I traveled with the ball club, sitting behind home plate charting pitches, making personal appearances—doing everything I could do for the club. I told Peter O'Malley, the owner of the Dodgers, "I can't pitch while I'm rehabbing, but I'll do anything to help out."

When players, coaches, and managers from other teams would all say to me, "Do you really think you're going to rehabilitate that arm to ever look like a pitching arm again?" I would answer them, "I sure am."

My recovery was a long, hard pull back—a year and a half of constant work every day but Sunday—but I did come back, pitching more games after the surgery than I had ever pitched before, playing for the Yankees, pitching for them in the World Series.

So many people just looked at me and shook their heads that I was bound and determined to give it my very best effort. Maybe it's my Welsh heritage, or whatever, but I enjoy proving people wrong.

THINK OF CHANGING YOUR ROLE IN THE GAME IF IT KEEPS YOU IN WHAT YOU LOVE.

So what if you have a setback?

In 1970, when seventeen-year-old Steve Mandl was a star pitcher at his high school in Brooklyn, he was invited to try out for the Mets at Shea Stadium. A shattered kneecap closed that door. Ten years later the door to baseball unexpectedly opened once again, this time in the form of a coaching job for George Washington High School in Washington Heights—a job that no one else would take and that he planned to keep only temporarily. In his words:

I picked up a bat and started hitting ground balls. Every-thing changed for me in that moment. I had a happiness I hadn't had in years—just hearing the ball hit the bat, seeing the kids running. They could see I knew my stuff. When I left that evening, I was walking on air. I thought, Why did I wait so long?

Sometimes when I'm coaching third base, I think to myself, I can't believe I'm here. I never thought I could

29

help anybody with anything. I was never the kid who wanted to be a fireman or a doctor. What did I care about anybody else? I was going to be a baseball player and get all the glory. Now I just want to do the job. Let the kids get the glory.

Mandl guided his team to the Manhattan division championship for seven straight seasons. For him getting back into baseball was more satisfying than he had ever imagined.

IT DOESN'T MATTER HOW MANY TIMES YOU FAIL, ALL YOU NEED IS ONE SUCCESS.

Many doors may close before the right one opens. Just look at the success story of Wess Roberts and his book, *Leadership Secrets of Attila the Hun:*

> *My book was turned down by seventeen publishers, but I had put so much work into it that I could not just let it die. I went ahead and had copies of it printed up at my own expense and eventually, by word of mouth, there was enough interest in it that I could no longer handle orders efficiently.*
>
> *Warner Books bought the rights and it went on to become one of the top ten best-selling titles for the year. Had I just been discouraged and thrown it over, the whole thing never would have come to fruition.*

"It takes twenty years to make an overnight success."
EDDIE CANTOR (1892–1964),
American comedian

PERSISTENCE PAYS OFF.

In the highly competitive art world, many an aspiring artist comes up against a wall in getting his or her work shown by a gallery. Kathy Wood, the mother of two school-age children and an enamelist who lives in the Princeton, New Jersey, area, gives a notable account of how persistence pays off:

> *I am part of a group of enamelists who had wanted to have a show of our work in the beautiful corporate gallery of Bristol-Myers Squibb, in Princeton. It is an important place for getting attention locally, and one of the major places to show in New Jersey.*
>
> *In 1985 we presented the woman who was in charge of the gallery with a portfolio of our work and she turned us down. This was a very definite closed door for us, because galleries plan years in advance and when you get turned down, you have to start all over again.*
>
> *Two years later, hearing that she had left, I proposed the show again, making no reference to our earlier rejection. I was told that the new person would not be starting the job for another six months, and that I should call her in the spring. Then the company underwent a big merger, and I was told I should call again in another few months, when things settled down. After a few appointments and*

31

cancellations we finally got to show the new director of the gallery and her assistant what we had, and they liked it very much but would not commit to a show. Over the next few months, not wanting to bug her by phone, I wrote the director several letters saying how much we'd love to discuss dates for the show, never once mentioning that there had not yet been a firm commitment.

Finally, just as we were about to give up, we got a call saying yes, the gallery had decided to give us a show. That was the day that clinched it, and we had our show in March 1991, more than six years after first approaching the gallery. We got a rave review in The New York Times, *coverage in the Newark* Star-Ledger *and all the local papers. The response was more than we'd ever hoped for—a great career push!*

DON'T TAKE A SILENT RESPONSE TO BE A NEGATIVE RESPONSE.

Dan Sullivan, former drama editor and theater critic of *The Los Angeles Times*, found this out the hard way:

If they say no, make sure it's definite and that they say it to your face. I once applied for a job, didn't hear back from the company, and took that to mean I'd been rejected. Years later I discovered that I had actually gotten the job, but my application had gotten lost and they didn't know how to reach me.

HOPELESSNESS IS A RELATIVE STATE.

Personal stories are a powerful inspiration when you are tempted to give up, but so are the collective efforts of whole populations to survive. As Rabbi Joseph Telushkin, author of *Jewish Literacy* and *The Nine Questions People Ask About Judaism*, illustrates, *hopelessness is a relative state:*

> In 1964 Look *magazine ran a cover story, "The Vanishing American Jew," predicting that the Jewish population of the United States would severely decrease by the year 2000. As my friend Michael Medved has noted, "It is now more than twenty-five years later. Look at the Jewish people, and look at* Look *magazine."*
>
> *If there was ever a time in Jewish history when one might have thought that the Jewish community was in danger of going out of existence, it was in the early 1940s. On many otherwise unexceptional days in 1942, 1943, and 1944, ten thousand or more Jews were murdered in Nazi death camps. By the time World War II ended in 1945, six million Jews, more than one third of world Jewry's population, were dead.*
>
> *Indeed, if that was the only fact one knew about Jewish life of the time, one would have been justified in assuming that either the end of the Jews was near, or that many, many decades would lapse until Jewry was again vibrant.*
>
> *But a corner was turned, very quickly. Within three years of the end of the Holocaust, Israel was established as a Jewish homeland and state. The emaciated Jews who*

survived the Holocaust, their families destroyed, their property stolen, flocked to Israel in large numbers. It is estimated that of the six thousand Jews who died in Israel's War of Independence—one percent of the country's population—at least half were survivors of the Nazi camps.

During the two thousand years in which the Jews were dispersed from their homeland, the Holocaust was the worst event that happened to them, and the creation of Israel the best. And the two events happened within three years of each other. It would seem that the old saw "One door closes, another door opens" can apply to nations as well as individuals.

Before you walk away dejectedly from a closed door, see if you can force it back open. If you see a crack, lean on it. Give that door a good hard push; throw your weight against it. Don't give up.

4

NOW WHAT?

If a door closes for good, don't fight it.

ACCEPT THE PROSPECT OF CHANGE.

That's the only way you can move ahead. Pat Riley, the head coach of the New York Knicks and the man who coached the L.A. Lakers basketball team to four championships in nine seasons, offers this valuable advice on accepting change:

> I was waived out of the NBA in 1976 as a player, and that left me outside of an industry I was part of for a long time, with relationships, friends, a place to go, and a job to do—all those things you need to feel part of something; to feel significant. I was pretty bitter and resented it, and I fought the change and went out and felt sorry for myself.
>
> However, once I stopped wallowing in self-pity, all of a sudden things began to happen for me. I got back into the game at a very low level, first as a traveling secretary, then as a broadcast commentator and analyst for the

Laker games, and within a year and a half I was signed as assistant coach. Within two years of that I was the head coach of the Lakers.

The only thing you can count on for being permanent in life is change, but many people fight it. They wait for the inevitable to happen instead of taking the initiative themselves to wrap it up, finish it correctly, say thank you and good-bye, and then move on without any kind of the bitter resentment or toxic feelings that only keep you down.

Sometimes you are forced to change because of things you can't control, other times you must go through an experience before you realize it is time to change and move on. Whatever the reason, I think we all know when the winds of change begin to blow; when the walls are beginning to close in—it is essential to listen to that voice inside. We need to see those moments in life for what they offer as a chance to step out and move on to something better. That's what life is all about and there's nothing wrong with that! Change can be wonderful if you move with it.

Absolutism in anything is ridiculous. You must stay open to the possibilities of a new affiliation or relationship. Embrace change, and great happiness is out there waiting for you.

EVERYTHING HAS A PURPOSE;
EVERYTHING HAS ITS OWN TIME.

Changes—doors closing, doors opening—actually occur all through life despite anything we do about them. Kathy Cronkite, author of *On the Edge of the Spotlight,* daughter of Walter Cronkite, and mother of two young children, describes how the most wonderful moments in life would certainly pass unappreciated if we fought the changes they wrought. In her words, there is no more beautifully or more frequently observed proof of this in life than in parenting:

As I sit here, I remember milestone after milestone of my two boys' lives, each a door closing and a door opening. Parenting, I realized as soon as William left the womb, is all about letting go. I vividly remember weeping as he began to teethe. I love that gummy little smile! I told myself; I don't want to lose that little smile.

Of course, each smile—two-toothed, fully toothed, or metallic—has its own sweetness. With each stage that I would delight in, I would anticipate the sadness of its ultimate passing. But as each new stage began, I would be so delighted with it that I never looked back and mourned what no longer was. I loved the baby's charming and inventive sign language and expressions as he tried so hard to communicate, but once he could ask questions and tell stories, we had even more fun together.

My nine-year-old leapt suddenly and unexpectedly out

of little-boyness, but how interesting it is to be able to discuss the Persian Gulf, or learn from him about RBIs and ERAs. No more beautifully illustrated bedtime picture books; now I'm being led to discover Robert Louis Stevenson, and I guess the phrase becomes One book closes, another opens.

DON'T DWELL ON WHAT COULD HAVE BEEN DONE DIFFERENTLY.

It's another way of resisting change, and it can only keep you down. This is especially true after the breakup of a personal relationship. Look at the assets you bring to a good relationship instead—for example, that you have what it takes to be a good friend, to listen, to see another person's side. This knowledge of yourself can help you move into a new and better relationship.

5

TAKE TIME OUT—
TO THINK!

*"A man should learn to detect and watch that gleam of light
which flashes across his mind from within, more than the
luster of the firmament of bards and sages."*
RALPH WALDO EMERSON (1803–1882),
American philosopher

*"Making a success of something has nothing to do with luck.
Care, thought, and study go into making something succeed;
luck is something you get playing the lottery, a roulette
game, or gambling."*
WESS ROBERTS
Author of Leadership Secrets of Attila the Hun

DON'T ALWAYS BLAME THE OTHER
FELLOW.

When a door closes, take the time to evaluate your
situation. If need be, change your attitude to make
new doors open.

What happened could have been your own fault;
next time, do it differently.

William Fromm, an expert in the field of advertising, promotion, and marketing, and the author of
*The Ten Commandments of Business and How to
Break Them,* shares a boyhood experience that
taught him an important lesson for life:

When I was about thirteen years old, growing up in Kansas City, I was in a Boy Scout troop. Scouts was a very big thing then; everyone participated. Within my troop the boys who were considered the leaders belonged to a special group called the Powder Horn. These boys were elected to the group by the scouts, the scoutmasters, the assistant scoutmasters—everybody participated in the vote and it was really a big deal. At age thirteen and almost an Eagle Scout, what you wanted most in life was to become a member of this special, elite group.

At the last troop meeting of the year, when it was announced who had been chosen for the Powder Horn for the next year, I found out I did not get in. All my friends got in, but for whatever reasons, I did not. I went home in tears and told my father what had happened. I had a list of my own reasons and rationalizations about why I wasn't picked—and why all of the rest of the troop was wrong in turning me down.

I did get in the next year, but the good that came out of that experience was my father's advice. Since the majority of members of the troop had decided who would get into the Powder Horn, "All I can tell you is this," he said, "if you are in a marching band and you are marching down the street and everybody is going 'left, right, left,' and you are going 'right, left, right,' you cannot assume they are all out of step."

This advice is something I've remembered when people don't react to me the way I want them to, or if something doesn't go the way I want it to. I start by assuming it is me who needs to adjust, rather than create an excuse about why things did not go my way.

Many people dismiss their ability to "think creatively" when a door closes. That kind of defeatist attitude is all wrong. Find ways to get your thinking out of a rut and new ideas will come.

TURN A SITUATION OVER AND OVER IN YOUR MIND UNTIL THAT NEW IDEA EMERGES.

Do this often enough and eventually you will make it a habit to see, hear, and think creatively. Past president of ASCAP, lyricist Hal David, whose hit songs include "Promises, Promises"; "Raindrops Keep Falling on My Head," "What the World Needs Now Is Love," shares a delightful story of how you can turn anything into an opportunity:

Ideas for songs come from everywhere. Some time ago I was working in London and was invited to a dinner party. The hostess told me that when I got to the house, don't bother ringing the bell, just walk in. "That will make it one less bell for me to answer," she said.

The line took hold of me and wouldn't let go. Burt Bacharach put it to music and a few years later, the 5th Dimension recording of "One Less Bell to Answer" became a big hit.

YES, YOU CAN DO ANYTHING YOU WANT TO DO.

Dr. Martin Katahn, psychologist, professor at Vanderbilt University, and author of several books on weight management including *The Rotation Diet*, which topped the best-seller lists in both hardcover and paperback when it was published in 1986, offers his own proof that by thinking the situation through you can turn luck, skill, and ingenuity into a winning combination.

I was born just before the Depression, to immigrant parents, and of course during those days, you had to try to look at the bright side of things and consider how to turn whatever happened into an opportunity. It didn't matter whether you succeeded or failed at an endeavor, as long as you kept looking for the opportunity it presented you to get better.

This philosophy, that you had to keep trying no matter what happened, went together with a very strong sense of self-reliance—that you looked to yourself for your strength, and to your family for moral support. Indeed, in those times there was no welfare, no Social Security, nobody to take care of you but yourself and your family.

As a result of my upbringing I always had the feeling I could do pretty much whatever I wanted to do—and I did. I had enough musical skills as a violinist that when I came to Nashville, I was quickly discovered and did backup music for just about every country-music star here. When I realized that a life on the road was not for me and I wasn't achieving the level of success that I wanted, even though I was a pretty good violinist, I went into the family business, selling refrigerators. When I decided I did not want to stand on my feet all day long and sell refrigerators, I went back to school and became a psychologist. I wrote my first book, The Two Hundred Calorie Solution, when I was fifty-three years old, with the encouragement of the people who had been in my classes. I'd never written a book before, just scientific articles, but that book led to a whole new career as a writer. I am now on my seventh book.

POLISHING YOUR IMAGE

When a door closes, take time out to groom yourself mentally and physically for new opportunity:

Take a personal inventory. |

Just as a company fills an inventory, so must an individual build a roster of positive qualities and personality traits that can be put to good use in any area of life. Put your head together with someone who knows you well, who can help you determine your pluses. Do you thrive on chaos? Enjoy being around people? What are your positive traits? Review your successes—how did you act or what did you do that made the success? Where or with whom have you been happiest and most confident? Why was it so? Everyone has areas where they can speak with authority and feel most confident about themselves.

When a door closes, ask yourself, what do I have from this situation or experience that I can use in a different, better way?

Add your answers to your personal inventory. Shape them into new ideas for making a change.

Strengthen your ability to communicate with others.

Stand tall, speak in a low tone, and don't be afraid to make eye contact. Avoid looking or sounding depressed, because that is a real turnoff. No matter how down you may feel, convey an upbeat attitude.

Don't let the fear of speaking to a group hold you back from making a good impression. In my own case this could have been an obstacle had I not been invited back to my alma mater, City College, to teach in the Business School. This was a great honor, but it was also a source of anxiety. Many people are afraid to speak in public, but for me it was more than this. As an undergraduate in the same college, my oral presentation was what caused me to be turned down in my bid for a teaching career. I had been invited back as a guest professor by the same school that, because of my diction, had closed a door on me!

On my first day of teaching I walked into the assigned classroom and it was filled to capacity with college students. I was so nervous, I dropped all the admission cards. Someone helped me pick them up (luckily no one laughed) and when I finally got to the front of the room I decided that the best way to calm down was to take attendance. I called out the name of each student listed on the cards slowly and calmly, so that by the time I had finished, I was speaking in a normal voice and could once again concentrate on what I'd planned to say.

After a few weeks of teaching I got over my nervousness and actually came to enjoy speaking in public, a skill that has served me well to this day.

Even if your "public" only consists of one or two people in a meeting, be prepared to make a good impression by what you have to say.

Envision your success in communicating your message, not your failure. Breathe freely, stand tall, and keep your body relaxed. Think before you speak. Look for opportunities to speak in a meeting, or to a group. Visibility in a crowd is a magnet for making new contacts and opening up new opportunities.

Improve your personal appearance.

People often get a low feeling about themselves because of their appearance, and that can stand in the way of making a good impression. If you sense there is room for improvement in how you look, do something about it so that you feel better about yourself. *How you see yourself is important because it reflects on how others see you.* Buy a new outfit, have your hair cut or restyled, be sure your shoes are in good shape and polished; keep your fingernails neat and clean. Sometimes all it takes is a small, inexpensive change in clothing and appearance to create confidence and make an impact.

While not advocating cosmetic surgery or more drastic measures, I believe there's nothing wrong with changing certain elements of your appearance if it improves your attitude about yourself. Again, how *you* see yourself is so important to the good impression you make.

> **Don't get hung up on appearance. If you feel good about yourself, you will make doors open.**

If you have trouble accepting yourself for who you are, be open to getting outside help. Otherwise, relax and accept your body image. Doctors note that people who improve their body image and self-esteem actually walk, talk, and even begin to think, differently.

**Don't let a weight problem
stand in your way of a new
opportunity.**

If you are overweight and unhappy about it,
chances are you are closing doors on yourself
in your personal or professional life. You can
keep your weight under control *if you put your
mind to it.*

Confront illness.

Don't let a doctor's dire predictions about your
health close the door on a happy, healthy life.
As Ted Isaac's story (see page 119) so dramati-
cally proves, many a doctor has been proven
wrong. Explore every way possible to open another door on improving your health. Get a second or even a third opinion, try a new therapy
or medication, and do everything in your
power to put up a fight and live life to the fullest.

**Do not become immobilized by
pain.**

Research the many new techniques available
for dealing with it, including surgery. "I would
make the choice again," says Edward Villella

about his hip replacement surgery that not only eliminated extreme pain but also allowed him to go on to become the artistic director of the Miami City Ballet. "I was angry at the idea that hip deterioration would make me retire," he said in *DanceMagazine*. "I lived with pain for over five years and then chose not to live with it any longer. Now I teach and demonstrate everything except big jumps, and have enough stamina to do whatever is necessary to direct or rehearse long hours."

TRY, STOP, AND THINK. THEN TRY AGAIN.

Struggling to launch a career as a theater director, Gordon Edelstein was so devastated by a door closing that he almost gave up. He just needed a better way in:

The pivotal moment in my profession involved one door closing, another door opening. For many years I had been doing a show here and there and, between shows, waitering and word-processing just to get by. I had been trying to make it as a theater director by working with new playwrights and new plays—riding the coattails of certain plays in order to further my career. In doing this I gave my life's blood to developing one play—hustling to get a theater to produce it; setting up readings, working with the author—I really believed in this play and gave it a year and a half of my life. Finally it got picked up by a theater, and the writer dropped me like a hot potato. My phone calls were not returned. I was suddenly treated as persona non grata by someone who I thought had become a good friend of mine. It was an enormously painful experience for me. I had been right in my belief about this play. It went on to national success and was optioned for a movie. It launched the career of this writer in theater and in film, while at the same time there I was, back at the restaurant.

I had worked so long and hard that when this experience happened, I really caved in. I quit the business over it. I started getting law school applications and considered going to graduate school in psychology.

And then in the aftermath of my colossal disappointment—in the process of leaving—I began to look inside myself and see all the ways in which I had been approaching the whole thing in a completely wrong way. I saw that I had in some ways participated in this disappointment, and in some ways had set myself up for it.

At the beginning of Edward Albee's play The Zoo Story there is a line about having to go out of your way a long way before coming back a short way, the right way. And for me that was true. I found a new way in—depending more on myself and less on others. That bottoming out was the beginning of what has been a very gratifying series of opportunities and successes that have brought great artistic satisfaction and many new challenges on the horizon. In 1991 I was asked by Arthur Miller to direct the one-act version of his new play The Last Yankee, which I did. I became the associate artistic director at the Long Wharf Theatre in New Haven, and *then, after* The Homecoming, *on Broadway, Harold Pinter asked me to direct his new play,* Party Time. *The first television film I directed,* Abby, My Love, *won the Humanities Award and was nominated for five Emmy Awards, including Best Director.*

The moment of being left behind in the wake of someone else's success became the turning point for me in more ways than one. Shortly after this I met my wife and everything changed for the good. It was a moment that related to all things in my life, leaving adolescence and moving on to adulthood. Latching on to one thing—that play—as a career per se was not anywhere near as useful as stepping back and standing alone on my own two feet.

LET HUMOR CUSHION THE BLOW.

There are many ways to give yourself some distance from a bad situation so you can keep going; one of the best is having a sense of humor, especially about yourself and your circumstances.

Abraham Lincoln was known for his sense of humor and wit, something that was never properly captured in the stiff, formal poses and long-exposure photography of his time. "I laugh because I must not weep," he once said; "that's all, that's all."

ARTHUR PINE

KEEP AN UPBEAT ATTITUDE AS YOU STRUGGLE THROUGH.

Let Beatrice Bernstein be your example. She's twice a widow and yet making the most of her life—visiting her children and grandchildren, studying, traveling, acting as a volunteer, and retaining a wonderful sense of humor:

> I am over the hill but I'm enjoying the downward slide. I've been a widow nearly nine years and have made a new life for myself that is full and exciting. My fellow students at Arizona State University, where I took courses, became my support group after my second husband died of colon cancer in 1982.
>
> Through the Elder Hostel program I have traveled around the world with people my own age who share my interests and need for companionship. The most worthwhile and rewarding project I have undertaken since retiring was a three-month stint in B'Nai B'Rith's Active Retirees in Israel (ARI) program. My special niche in the program was to serve as "resident bubbe" (grandmother) in an Orthodox day-care center in Netanya. My charges were the pitzelach, the little ones ages eighteen months to three years. True, it was noisy and tiring at times, but the need I filled and the love I was able to give and receive gave me a high that was positively illegal!

When friends conveyed good wishes that Mrs. Bernstein reaches *me'ah ve'esrim,* 120 years, she commented, "I may just make it. Only forty-four years to go!"

6

KEEP MOVING!

*"The choice is between doing something and doing nothing,
and doing nothing never gets you anywhere."*
FELIX G. ROHATYN,
American financier

*"You can commit no greater folly than to sit by the roadside
until someone comes along and invites you to ride with him
to wealth or influence."*
JOHN B. GOUGH (1817–1886),
American temperance lecturer

Different people react differently when a door closes on them. Some are disgusted; others want revenge. Some will be inspired to show that the person or organization who closed the door was wrong; others will be enveloped in sadness and despair.

TAKE ACTION!

Whatever your initial reaction, *you must take action* if you are ever going to move ahead. You can't let rejection get you down.

The former prime minister of Great Britain Margaret Thatcher was interviewed by Barbara Walters and asked how she felt when she was voted out of office. Mrs. Thatcher replied that it was just something to be faced and that she had to move on. She said it was awful to leave Number Ten Downing Street within five days, after having been there for eleven years, suddenly without secretarial help, office space, expense allowance. She said that though it was tough, she had made up her mind to face the facts as they are and move forward. Her friends loaned her office space and secretarial help and she quickly regained her old spirit, never letting that closed door keep her down for long.

People are not born optimists or pessimists; it is the attitude they assume that forms their outlook. You are the one who makes that determination.

You have been knocked down; now you must choose how you react. Will you stay down on the mat for the count of ten? In boxing the longer you stay down, the harder it is to get up. Will you bounce up and go forward? The same punch that knocks the passive fighter flat causes the fighter who is determined to win to fall back momentarily before regaining his balance. Remember Newton's law: For every action there is a reaction.

YOUR BIGGEST BREAK CAN COME FROM NEVER QUITTING.

As Dinah Shore discovered when she was trying to break into show business, being at the right place at the right time can only happen when you keep moving toward the next opportunity:

> I did not get that job I wanted so badly, to sing with Benny Goodman's orchestra, even though I felt I really sang my little heart out at the audition. Someone told me they were auditioning girls for a solo spot on a local radio station in New York called WNEW. I ran over—auditioned—got the job, a new first name and, not too much later, that "BIG BREAK" on the Eddie Cantor variety show because his daughter Marjorie heard me sing on WNEW!

It may take several changes before landing solidly on your feet, but do not give up.

AN UNHAPPY SITUATION MAY BE YOUR BACK DOOR TO SUCCESS.

Jack Smith's career at *The Los Angeles Times* as a columnist is a perfect example of keeping up the momentum until you find your niche. In his words:

After the war I worked three years at the old Daily News *and three years at the* Herald-Express. *Then I went back to the* News *but stayed only three months. I was disenchanted with newspaper pay, and when a national public relations firm offered me a substantial increase, I quit and took the job, in the Los Angeles bureau. I hated it. After a six-month trial I quit, just in time, I'm sure, to avoid being fired. I was without a job or a prospect.*

A friend told me the city editor of the Times *wanted to talk to me. I went to work for the* Times *in June 1953. Five years later I was writing a column three days a week. In 1970 I was made a full-time columnist, writing five days a week.*

Except for illness I have never missed a deadline since. I have written eight books derived from my column. I have had a rewarding career.

If I hadn't bombed in public relations, I would still be an unhappy flack.

USE THE FEELING OF DEFEAT AS YOUR MOTIVATION TO GET OUT OF A BAD SITUATION.

"I knew I didn't want to have that feeling again," said Michael Jordan, star of the world champion Chicago Bulls, in describing the tears he cried when it looked like the door to basketball was closed to him.

In fact, it was those tears that gave him the determination to keep doors open on the game he loved. It happened when he was a sophomore in high school in Wilmington, North Carolina. Confident that he'd make the team, Jordan discovered that his name was not posted on the list in the school gym. "I thought that if I didn't stop looking, my name would be there, but I wasn't there," he said; at the end of the school day he went home, closed the door to his room, and cried. It didn't take long for him to snap out of it. He cried again when he told his mother, but that was it. From there Jordan worked on his playing skills, trying harder than ever. Nature assisted him. He grew from five feet ten inches to an agile six feet two inches, and the next year made the team. The rest is basketball history.

DON'T LET DEFEAT FLATTEN YOU.

It is hard to imagine James Patterson, CEO of J. Walter Thompson North America, and a best-selling author, in a hopeless situation. However, there were several times in his life when such a situation occurred—one in particular that served as prime motivation for pushing him on to something better:

When I first came to New York I had literally no money. I was living in a hotel on Fifty-first Street between Tenth and Eleventh avenues, for twenty-eight dollars a week, I think it was, in a tiny room that actually had a blinking cross outside the window—the kind of thing you see in all those bad movies. The walls in this little room were covered with a dingy wallpaper that consisted of a very intricate pattern of thousands of little pendants repeated over and over again, and in each of those little pendants, throughout the entire room, someone had penciled an X.

This was my hopelessness. I knew I had to find a job to get me out of this situation, and I did everything I could possibly do to line up interview after interview. Just when I thought I'd landed a job on Wall Street, at the last minute, for some reason, I didn't get it.

You can't imagine—well, maybe you can—how I felt when I knew I had to go back to that room and stare at those pendants in the wallpaper again.

Two days later I was hired at J. Walter Thompson, and that turned out to be the best thing that could have happened to me, moving up through the ranks to become CEO of North America.

Find a focal point in your situation (such as that hopeless wallpaper described above), and use it as motivation to find a way out.

USE A BAD SITUATION TO OVERCOME OTHER OBSTACLES IN YOUR LIFE.

Tough times become like gym equipment. Just ask anyone who has weathered the worst: it makes you tougher.

"Whenever I have a problem I can look back to the low point in my life and say, my God, I came through that okay! What I'm confronted with now is far less than that, and so I'll get through this, or that, also."
WALLY AMOS,
Entrepreneur

GIVE YOURSELF A SECOND CHANCE.

Lyricist Sammy Cahn—whose hit songs include "Come Fly with Me," "It's Magic," "Love and Marriage," and "Three Coins in the Fountain"—provides wonderful examples from his professional and personal life of how that second chance is out there waiting for you if you will only pick yourself up and go toward it:

For me the most traumatic experiences of my life were the result of doors closing.
At an early stage in my career I was let go by the Warner Music Company after being salaried for years

61

and years. There I was, the sole support of my parents and four (count 'em, four!) sisters, without a job. I truly believed it was the end of my career—but it was actually the start! I went on to write songs, and from that day to this have been self-employed. (I couldn't have a nicer boss than me!)

The second door closing for me was the failure of my first marriage. After eighteen (count 'em, eighteen!) years of what I'd thought was a perfect life, it suddenly ended.

I was a man haunted by the very ballads he had written. But another door opened in the person of my present wife, Tita. We have been married for over twenty years and life could not be better. I don't live by lyrics, but the words I wrote about love being more satisfying "The Second Time Around" suit my life perfectly.

7

TELL YOUR STORY

When a door closes, don't run away and hide.

**SHARE YOUR SITUATION WITH
SOMEONE WHO VALUES YOUR TALENT.
ASK FOR THEIR HELP.**

Red Holzman, NBA Hall of Fame inductee and the man who coached the New York Knicks basketball team to two NBA championships, did not hesitate in his hour of need to "call Fuzzy"—one of his oldest and closest friends:

When I was coach of the St. Louis Hawks, about a third of the way into the season the owner of the team decided to make a change in coaching—in other words, get rid of the coach. He was probably right because the team was not doing all that well, but it was the first time I was fired from anything, and I felt terrible. That's the end of basketball, I figured; no more basketball.

So I went back to New York, not really knowing what I would do next, and got in touch with my friend Fuzzy Lavaine, who had just been made head coach of the Knicks. I asked Fuzzy to help me out and he hired me to take over his old position—I became a scout for the Knicks. If I had not just picked up and left St. Louis, he would have hired someone else, but there I was in New York and I took that job thinking it would only be an interim job and nothing more. I really did not feel as if I would ever coach again—or want to.

After I had been a scout for a while it turned out that by circumstance I was made an interim coach, and from there I became a coach, and then general manager, and I was with the Knicks for about fourteen years. We had a good team. We won a couple of championships and I was elected into the Basketball Hall of Fame, a dream every-body has.

Coaching the Knicks for a good number of years and being associated with a lot of wonderful people in a first-class outfit—Fuzzy gave me the opportunity to do that and it turned out to be a great break for me. It was a great career and a lot of fun, especially since the Knicks' home was my home, New York.

For Wally Amos, the talented entrepreneur, creator of the Famous Amos cookie, and author, the solution to a bad situation was also but a phone call away:

One of the dark moments in my life that I got through with flying colors occurred just after my wife, Shirley, had given birth to our son, and we moved to California. I had left my job as an agent with the William Morris

Agency in New York to set up a whole entertainment complex in Los Angeles—a recording company, a management company, and a publishing company. This was my ultimate dream and while I knew it would take time, it was well under way toward coming true. One of my partners in the venture was Hugh Masekela, a South African musician and vocalist.

At the time, he was my client and a big up-and-coming star. One of his records was coming up on the charts; I was making contacts and booking dates for him and doing all the things that I do well—for that December I had booked him on an eight-day tour for which he would receive about eleven thousand dollars—more money than he had ever earned.

The first day home from the tour Masekela called me and said, "Wally, we need to talk. Can I come over?"

Great! I thought, we'll review the tour, discuss new plans; I was really looking forward to it. Instead of a good thing, however, that meeting turned out to be a disaster. Masekela told me he thought I wasn't handling his career properly and he no longer wanted me to represent him. He was very definite about it.

Masekela's news could not have come at a worse time. That very morning I had put Shirley in a hospital; she was suffering from nervous exhaustion. She was totally worn out from the move, the baby, and all the changes we'd undergone, and so there I was, with a wife in a hospital, a three-month-old son, no source of income, and the whole reason why I'd moved to California suddenly nonexistent.

Without a doubt this was one of the lowest points in my life, but I did not let it last for long. Since I am one of those who believe you're never going to solve a problem unless you come up with a solution, I moved quickly into gear to do just that.

Only a few weeks before this I had gotten a call from my friend John Levy, a big-time manager who represented Cannonball Adderley, Nancy Wilson, Joe Williams, and many others, who had wanted me to come work with him. My response at the time had been, "John, I really appreciate the offer and I'm flattered that you want me to join you, but things have never been better for me than they are now and I just have to stay put."

This time I called him and said, "Hey, John, about that job . . ." Sure enough, that job was still there waiting for me and I was with John for a while and one thing led to another, and life went on. My wife got back on track; my son is a grown man and happily married, and life is beautiful.

INCREASING YOUR CONTACTS

"Who you know" and who you can contact counts for a lot when a door closes. Your connections with others can open new doors in unexpected ways. Spend time now to prepare for that time when you must ask for help in making a new door open:

Cultivate a genuine interest in other people.

You don't become friends with a person just for connections they might have, but you never know when such a friendship will open up a door.

Many of the friendships I developed when I did publicity for show-business personalities led to new business when I became a literary agent representing, for example, such celebrities as George Burns, Bob Hope, Milton Berle, and Jack Benny's daughter, who came to me through a good friend who was a personal manager in show business.

> **Look for ways to help others when they need it, and go out of your way to help them.**

Do this not for what they may owe you later on, but rather because they are down and out and need a lift. There's probably no more memorable or moving example of this wisdom than Frank Capra's movie classic *It's a Wonderful Life,* starring James Stewart and Donna Reed. With his home-loan business in ruins, he is contemplating suicide so that his insurance policy will bail his family out, but then the character played by James Stewart is ultimately saved by the hundreds of people he has helped over the years in his small town. They need but one call from his wife that "George needs help" and out they come, thronging into his home with small donations of cash.

Show yourself to be a generous, upbeat person at all times, understanding of other people's problems and ready to lend a hand.

You will probably meet the same people on your way up as you do on your way down, when you find yourself in a closed-door situation. The people you've helped on the way up will go out of their way to be helpful to you when a door closes and you need them!

Conversely, if you put people off with a negative, irritable, or downbeat manner, you cannot expect them to lend a helping hand when you need it, or to recommend you to someone else who might improve your business situation. Your manner and attitude count just as strongly as your ability to give a good performance.

Show your appreciation for favors, large and small.

Not only with an outright thank-you to those who help you or *attempt* to help you in any way, but also by staying in touch and keeping them up-to-date on your progress with the leads or ideas they give you. It is very satisfying to know you have helped someone—give that satisfaction in return for assistance.

Never end a relationship on a sour note or with an argument.

Not only does it leave tension in the air to end on a sour note, but you may also be required to deal with that same person in the future. This is especially true in business, where the person who fired you may have been forced to do so, or the situation was out of his or her control. Venting your anger on that individual only increases bad feelings all around. Use your judgment, not your emotions, in deciding the time and place for your anger.

Go out of your way to end on a positive note.

When I worked in public relations and an account would terminate, the situation was really no different from being fired from a job—I lost work and income. However, in the end, I never took it personally. I knew I had done my best for the client, and I made sure we parted company on good terms. Had it been on a sour note, we'd probably never have done business again; whereas in fact, for one reason or another, many of the clients who left us ended up returning.

Associate with upbeat people.

Misery may love company, but it will never prove to be an inspiration to getting ahead. Grouchiness always proves to be an obstacle, as does the outlook of doom and depression that some people convey. Stay away from such people. Their approach to life can be catching! An upbeat attitude will be a plus at all times, but particularly when your objective is making a good impression. You may not *feel* upbeat, but try acting it anyway. You will be surprised at how quickly your bad mood is dispelled.

Circulate among people in your industry.

Be seen. If you were a major automobile manufacturer and you suddenly got a bad rating that could adversely affect your sales, you would quickly increase your advertising budget by a few million dollars to convey the message of how fine your car really is. As an individual you cannot afford to do that, of course, but when a door closes on you in business or in some other situation, the smartest thing to do is get out there and circulate among people in your industry and let them know you are on your feet and available for work. Write letters to the appropriate people. Make phone calls to anyone you know who might be able to use your services. Don't go into a shell like a turtle; rather, go out more than ever before and be seen. Don't be embarrassed to mingle with people in your field because you may be unemployed or recently demoted within your firm.

**When you contact people
you have not seen or spoken
to in quite a while, don't just
call them out of the blue to
ask them for a favor.**

When you call them, be prepared to invite them to lunch, catch up with what's going on in their life, and in return for their time and favors, offer them *your* help in some specific area. Come prepared with specific ideas in this regard—people you know or suggestions you might have that can enhance their situation. Look for ways you can reciprocate favors.

**Choose wisely whom you
take into your confidence.**

Don't publicly vent your negative opinions of other people; you never know if your words will get back to them. Keep your private thoughts to yourself unless you feel you must air them, in which case, let them go no farther than your spouse or closest friend.

SHOW 'EM YOU CAN DO IT!

This is what the great comedian Henny Youngman did when he picked up the phone in his hour of need. Taking matters into his own hands turned out to be the best thing that could have happened to him:

> I was with an agency once where I loaned money to the agents. I tried to get the money back but they never paid me. Instead, they turned the whole office on me. When I went up to collect what they owed me, I was told that if I did not forget about the money, I would not get any work from them.
>
> I walked out of that office and I wanted to jump out the window—I had a family to feed. I picked up a trade paper, and saw the name Sid Schwartz. Sid Schwartz, I thought; I used to know a guy by that name—he was booking a hotel, the Monte Carlo in Miami. I took a chance, and I called him.
>
> "Sid," I started to say, but he interrupted me. "Henny, can you put in two weeks for me? Twenty-five hundred a week?" He was offering me a job.
>
> "I'll look in the book," I told him, and called him back and picked up five thousand dollars' worth of work.
>
> Back to the paper, and now I see another agency booking the Thunderbird in Las Vegas. Two new guys. I got them on the phone and said, "I called up to wish you guys luck." And I meant it.
>
> "Mr. Youngman, we want to book you in for three weeks, five thousand a week. Can you do it?" They were

excited, and so was I. Suddenly, there was fifteen thousand dollars more money.

Before I got off the phone that day, I had fifty thousand dollars' worth of work booked. I waited until I had the contracts for those jobs in my hand, and then I went back up to the agency office where I had been treated so badly and I asked for my contract back; I tore it up. I showed them the contracts I'd gotten for myself—how they'd lost five thousand dollars' worth of commissions.

I've been doing it ever since, getting my own jobs.

Now, I was well known, but still, it took my getting on the phone and booking myself before I got the work.

BAD NEWS? SHARE IT!

You'd be surprised at how people can help if you just let them know your situation.

Little did Metropolitan Opera baritone Robert Merrill expect that by airing his misery—in his case, to a complete stranger—he would quickly alleviate it.

> I had been recording exclusively with RCA Victor for fifteen years when, totally out of the blue, they decided not to have any exclusivity contracts—my contract was over. I was depressed about this because it was a great company, and I did very well with them.
>
> After I got the bad news, I left the Victor offices and went to the Russian Tea Room, where I sat mulling over

my fate in a friendly atmosphere. Sitting next to me was an Artists and Repertoire man for London Records. "Bob, Bob!" he called out, describing how he recognized me and just had to say hello because he was a fan of mine. He sat down and we chatted, and I told him my sad story. "You know something—that's great!" he said. "We're casting the Lucia di Lammermoor album with Joan Sutherland. Would you do it with us?"

"Of course I would! I'd love to," I told him, and I went ahead and did that recording, and after that I did several more albums for London, and all of them turned out to be very big sellers—Kismet with Mantovani, an album called The Americana, which is now out on CD, and Lucia.

I got my great break with London Records because I was shut out of RCA Victor. If I hadn't gone to the Russian Tea Room to cry over a beer, and if I hadn't told my story to the London A & R man, I never would have gotten that wonderful contract with London.

KEEP UP YOUR FRIENDSHIPS AND CONTACTS.

A steady, friendly rapport will ultimately serve you well. William Fromm describes how an account shake-up in his advertising and marketing business proved that *business may change, friendships do not:*

> We represented a computer company that really took off after we got involved with it—we'd come up with a great ad campaign and it looked as if it was going to be a big account for our advertising firm. We'd been working hard, producing a clever television spot emphasizing the long-term reliability and staying power of this computer company, and had just gotten it approved when all of a sudden, on April first, I got a call from the president saying that the company had just been sold to a new owner who already had an advertising agency and they no longer needed us. At first I thought it was an April Fools' joke, but it wasn't. It was very tough news to accept, not only from a revenue standpoint but also because I'd developed really strong relationships with the people in the advertising division—in particular with the VP of marketing and the advertising manager.
>
> The business went away, but we did not lose out on everything—we hired the advertising manager to come over into our account services department and this turned out to be a great move because he knew the computer industry very well and could help us replace what business we had lost.

I kept up with the VP of marketing, even after he left the company, and he ended up as the president of Sears Business Centers, which today is one of our largest clients, a much larger account than that first one ever was, in size and sales.

Keep up your contacts; reach out to others. It's all right to ask for help. People are more willing to help than you might think.

8

GET MAD!

"Temperate anger well becomes the wise."
PHILEMON *(370–260 B.C.),*
Athenian comic poet

When a door closes, use constructive anger as a positive force to open new doors.

AM I EVER GOING TO SHOW THEM THEY MADE A MISTAKE.

That's the attitude to take when a door closes on you. Let it fire you up to work harder, to move ahead faster, to prove to those people, that firm, that lost friend or lover that through your next success they are going to regret ever having parted ways.

Academy Award–winning film producer David Brown, whose long list of credits includes *Jaws, The Sting,* and *Driving Miss Daisy,* describes how such vindication helped him and his partner reach the pinnacle of success in their fabulous movie-making collaborations:

When Richard Zanuck and I were fired from 20th Century–Fox on New Year's Eve of 1970, we couldn't realize that this was possibly the best thing that ever happened to our careers. We had been in a dispute with Darryl F. Zanuck and were forced out by the board of directors. As a result of being forced out we became producers and for the next eighteen years were responsible for films that not only made us independently wealthy but also, and more importantly, were nominated for and won Academy Awards, culminating in our receiving the highest honor awarded by the Academy of Motion Picture Arts and Sciences, the coveted Irving G. Thalberg Award.

For years we fantasized giving an acceptance speech at the Oscars in which we thanked the board of directors of 20th Century–Fox, declaring that without their firing us we probably would not be onstage to receive this honor.

In a somewhat different way the I'll-show-them attitude motivated member of Parliament Jeffrey Archer to take his first step toward an extraordinary career in publishing.

In August 1974, facing financial ruin and subsequent resignation from a promising career as a Conservative member of Parliament, Archer was lunching alone in a pub, mulling over his fate, when he overheard a nearby conversation about some "fool" who'd made a bad investment. "Oh, well, we're never going to hear about him again" was the final comment before the topic was dropped. Archer knew they were talking about him. He jumped up and left his lunch behind, swearing to himself, *"You will hear from me again."*

Fateful words, from one of the top-selling novelists of all time, driven to write books to beat off the creditors and right his reputation. "Many of us don't know what we can do until we are forced to do it," comments Archer. At the apex of success he could savor sweet revenge.

LET "HEALTHY HURT" KEEP YOU GOING.

There is no way you can stay down for long if you're angry and doing something about it.

Dan Sullivan, drama and theater critic, once again making a contribution to these pages, describes how he became a pro at honing anger into a fine-edged tool that made new doors open:

One of the best things that ever happened to me was not being appointed editor of our college literary magazine. That got me so mad that I went over to join the college paper, whose editor had wanted me on the staff for some time. Without that experience I doubt I would have gone into journalism.

Again, I was so mad at the Columbia School of Journalism for not accepting me for graduate school that I

*resolved to go as far away from home as possible—
Minnesota. That gave me a much more varied appren-
ticeship than if I had stayed in the East, and eventually I
ended up at* The New York Times *anyway.*

*I have found that it is very stimulating to have a door
shut in your face. It forces decisions. Either you say,
"Well, okay then, that's ruled out. I don't have to worry
about that anymore." Or you vow to show the guy who
closed the door that this was the worst mistake he
ever made in his life. No beats maybe as a goad to action
every time.*

Use your constructive anger to vindicate the closing of a door. Don't look for scapegoats or place
blame, but express your anger as a way to rid your
system of toxic feelings. New doors will open in the
process.

9

TRY ANYTHING!

"Great dreams are often so far away from your reach that you can become discouraged. But each small goal you achieve gives you confidence to try the next."
JOHN H. JOHNSON (b. 1918),
Publisher,
Ebony *magazine*

Go in with an open mind and find out for yourself whether a new opportunity exists.

IT'S NEVER TOO LATE TO MOVE AHEAD.

Although he hated to have it happen this way, George Burns explains how a door opened for him with the death of his best friend, Jack Benny:

> *Jack had been signed to play the lead with Walter Matthau in the movie version of* The Sunshine Boys, *by Neil Simon. About a month before the picture was to begin production, Jack took ill, and within a month passed away.*
>
> *Jack and I had been the best of friends right up until the end, and I knew his producer and manager, Irving Fein, very well.*
>
> *Irving approached Herb Ross, the director of* The Sunshine Boys, *and Neil Simon, with the idea that they use me in the part Jack was to play. At that time I was*

in my eighties and more or less semiretired, as I had been ever since my wife Gracie had passed away. I hadn't done a movie in thirty-five years.

The film people were afraid that because of my age I'd forget my lines and it would slow down production of the film, but Irving convinced them to give me the role.

About a week before going into production the director called for a reading of the screenplay with the members of the cast. When Irving and I arrived, everyone was sitting around a table, ready to read their parts and get some tips from Neil Simon and Herb Ross as to how to play them. Everybody had brought their scripts to the reading except me. The director and producer took Irving Fein to the side and said, "Irving, I don't think we should have signed George up for this. He doesn't even have his manuscript with him. He's already forgotten that he should have had it with him for today's cast reading."

Irving reassured them. "Please, don't worry; just get started with the rehearsal."

And so we got started, and a few minutes into the rehearsal everyone turned to me in amazement. Not only had I memorized my part but I knew everybody else's part by heart too.

"George, you don't even have your script. How are you doing this?" Walter Matthau asked me.

"Doing what? What's the big deal?" I said.

I really did have the whole thing memorized. It was a skill I had used as a child, to hide my humiliation at having trouble reading. Long before they'd found a name for it, I'd suffered from dyslexia. Later, in vaudeville, that skill of memorizing had served me well. Timing was everything to the performance, and knowing everyone's lines ensured perfect timing.

Anyway, I took over Jack's role in The Sunshine Boys

and won an Academy Award as Best Supporting Actor for my part in it. And I went on to do about ten movies after that.

Making the best use of every moment of his life, George Burns is a great example of a person who will try anything. His return to the center of the film limelight established him as an American legend. Somewhere up there Jack Benny must be smiling at having given George the opportunity for his late-in-life success.

GIVE YOURSELF ROOM FOR LETTING SOMETHING BETTER COME OF A BAD SITUATION.

Filmmaker Ross McElwee never realized that a broken love affair could change his life:

The success of my film Sherman's March *happened because something went wrong. In 1981 I received a small arts foundation grant to make a film about the lingering effects of Sherman's March on the South, over one hundred years after the event. I made all the preparations to begin the film when, just days before I was to leave for the South, I broke up with my girlfriend in New York. I was depressed and devastated by this event. It changed everything, and yet because I had*

85

planned to go shoot this documentary, I went on down South anyway to North Carolina where my family is, taking my filming equipment with me and just shooting things that interested me that had nothing to do with my original intention. The more I experimented with my camera, the more I started to realize that there was a theme I was interested in developing, which was my family's interest in securing a happy love relationship for me.

In the wake of this disastrous love affair that I had had in New York, everyone kept suggesting that I try to meet a nice southern girl.

I began filming little random moments of people talking to me about this; I even filmed my parents introducing me to a young woman who was the daughter of their friend. She became the first portrait in the film, and the film went on to be a series of encounters with southern women that I filmed on the road, true to the original intent of the film, retracing the route of Sherman's March through the South. In at least a nominal way it did end up being about Sherman's effect on the South—there is historical information contained in the film about Sherman—but it's much more a treatment of a personal journey through the South that I took. The film became, as a subtitle reads, "Meditations on the Possibilities of Romantic Love in the South During an Era of Nuclear Weapons Proliferation."

I had no idea of what I was doing when I began shifting the focus and theme of the film, but as it turned out, the film I made was probably much more interesting than the film I had set out to make, and to my great surprise it turned out to be a film that was seen very widely and received a lot of acclaim.

An awful lot of it was luck. First bad luck and then

extraordinary good luck in encountering situations that made it a very different kind of film. The original grant had given me seed money, and when I came back with this very different creature than I had originally started out to capture, foundations that I showed it to subsequently loved what I had.

The film changed my life. I had been plodding along making these films that were well reviewed but basically not shown widely outside of museums. And suddenly I had this film that was so strange and unusual, and humorous, I guess, that it received the kind of attention that documentary films very seldom get. It made all sorts of "ten best" lists, which at least enables a film to get the attention it needs to be seen, and it was seen, all across the country. It made money. I got calls from all the major studios asking if I wanted to write or direct in Hollywood. It enabled me to make the films I wanted to make, on my own schedule.

All of it happened because something went wrong, which is when it really helps to have a kind of Zen attitude toward things. In other words, if you concentrate too hard on trying to achieve something, sometimes it won't happen. For whatever reason, I was willing to completely abandon the original premise of the film and open up to something else—but that wouldn't have happened if I had not broken up with this woman in New York. I had to give myself over to what was unexpected and run with it.

BELIEVE IN YOUR ABILITIES. TRY SOMETHING NEW AND DIFFERENT AND YOU WILL MAKE IT.

Ann Miller's upbeat attitude and self-confidence proved invaluable when her film career with MGM came to an end.

When MGM fell and Mr. Mayer died, none of the contract players were ever re-signed. One by one, production chief Dore Schary let their contracts run out. When my time came up, I was very upset—I'd been under contract for twelve years to MGM and I felt like a fish out of water. However, one door closes, another door opens, and for me, that meant turning to "stage," working with a company of Mame in Palm Beach at the Royal Poinsettia Playhouse. I was such a big hit in it that the director contacted composer Jerry Herman to come in from New York to see me in the show. Mame was ready to close in New York, but Herman decided to put me in it and even though I was the sixth Mame to play the part, I was a smash hit!

The feeling Ann Miller had of being a "fish out of water" will be familiar to anyone who has ever had an unexpected change in their career.

DON'T LET EGO STAND IN YOUR WAY.

Advertising executive Michael Newbrand found that putting ego aside—in his case accepting a job in a smaller market than he had envisioned for himself—can open the door to a great new opportunity.

At the point when I lost my job, my whole world turned upside down. I am one of those tradition-bound people who married my high school sweetheart, and for our entire married life we lived seven miles from where we both grew up. I started as a summer job employee with Ogilvy and Mather during college in the 1960s and stayed with them, progressing up the ladder until 1989. At that point the company was sold and there was a wholesale adjustment within the organization, downsizing and cost-cutting, and after having been there since 1963 the message to me all of a sudden was: You were great last year but times have changed and there isn't a future for you here.

Needless to say, I felt shocked by the circumstances but very confident that other opportunities within the same industry and the same market would immediately come to pass.

That did not occur for a variety of reasons. Advertising was in an unhealthy period and the economy was beginning to slow down. I accepted an offer to go to Chicago, with Foote, Cone and Belding. My intentions were to have that be the new door for me and my family. However, the economy continued to get worse and we were unable to sell our home in New Jersey, and therefore couldn't make that happen. I came back to New York even more committed to making it in the city.

And then purely by happenstance—through contacting lots of people and sending out lots of information—I was contacted by a recruiter in Atlanta who asked me whether I had interest in talking to the Martin Agency, in Richmond, Virginia.

To be honest, I didn't, but I said, Fine, I'll talk to anybody.

And it turned out I discovered a whole new world. I liked the people I met at the agency; I found they had a vision and a plan, and I could see immediately that the opportunity for me to work for a smaller market was a great one, contributing twenty-odd years of experience across a wide array of clients to a two-hundred-man office instead of a five-hundred- to one-thousand-man office.

I also found that you can adjust very nicely to a new lifestyle. Because of the difference in the cost of living, we were able to drop the price of our home in New Jersey, buy a newer home that we like a whole lot better. It takes only twenty minutes to get to work, my family is happy with the move.

What was a very traumatic experience, I can see as I sit here now with it all having passed, has turned out like that old cliché—everything works out for the best. In my case it seems to be what I should have done a long time ago.

LISTEN TO OTHERS, BUT MAKE UP YOUR OWN MIND.

Friends or former employees may say, "Oh, that company is awful to work for; they demand too much from you," et cetera, but don't be influenced by them. Go in for that interview with your eyes and ears open; find out for yourself about the job. As Michael Newbrand found, it may be the best thing that ever happened to you. In the end let your own final judgment be the determining factor as to whether an opportunity exists.

The story of how film producer Mervyn LeRoy lost *Gone With the Wind* proves what can happen if you lose sight of this. Returning home to California from a business trip in New York, Mervyn LeRoy gave the manuscript for the book to his wife to read over the course of their three-day railroad trip west. When they got to Los Angeles, he asked her opinion and she gave it—that the book was "just another Civil War story; you've seen dozens of them and read dozens of them," she said to her husband. After listening to his wife Mr. LeRoy sent the manuscript back to the agent, and his rival, David O. Selznick, ended up with one of the greatest money-making movies of all time.

Everyone's entitled to an opinion but that,

undoubtedly, was the last time Mervyn LeRoy gave his lovely wife, Kitty, a manuscript to read!

The same holds true in your personal life, meeting new people. Of course it's great if everyone else sees what you see in a person you care about, but that is not always the case. You may see potential in a new relationship while others may tell you you're trading down or getting yourself into a bad situation. Don't always let the negative comments of friends or family influence your feelings. In their eyes there may never be anyone good enough for you, which in itself is like having a door stay closed on you before you even get the chance to open it. Go out with that person and judge for yourself. In spite of what others may have predicted, you might just hit it off and have wonderful times together.

SOLVING PEOPLE PROBLEMS

|Be willing to let things go.

When you find yourself at an impasse or about to get into an argument, stop and think before you blow off steam.

If you should have an argument with a friend or business associate or someone you care about, and that argument results in your breaking up the relationship, it's the same thing as having a door close.

Put yourself in the other person's shoes. Go back to that person and be ready to apologize. Never be ashamed to say "I'm sorry. It was my fault."

Such a move on your part may open the door again to a new relationship, better than the one before, that will cement the friendship.

Hold back on making judgments.

Go in with an open mind and find out for yourself whether a new opportunity exists—whether you can work with someone or not.

In our literary agency there are times when an author who has been represented by another agent will ask if we'd be interested in representing them. There are many reasons why this can happen, but for us, personal reasons have got to be the cause of the breakup—that the client did not get along personally with the agent, or that there was something specific in the relationship that caused it to founder. If that's the case, we'll think about it and call the other agent to discuss openly what the person is like and why they are splitting.

Sometimes we hear that the person is fine, but other times the agent tells us the author is tough to work with and never satisfied. This is where we try to keep an open mind. When we have this sort of negative reaction, we will sometimes take a gamble with the author because we respect their ability. We try to form our own opinions, and it often turns out that we get along fine. We've successfully represented such clients for years and years. We are not, however, the kind of agents who will ever "steal" an author from another agent. Life is too short to ever act in such a manner.

Don't let difficult people hold you back from opportunity.

Have you ever been frightened by someone you would like to work with but you did not know how to approach them? Don't let the fact that you must deal with a difficult person close the door on a new opportunity that you know is there waiting for you. If you can overcome the personality problem, the relationship could turn out to be a big asset.

> **Keep up your courage when it comes to dealing with difficult people.**

You may be tested severely—at the very same time that you are given the chance to accomplish your goals.

> **Find ways to release tension. Make people receptive to what you want to say to them.**

Some of the smartest, most talented people who bring you success can be tough, difficult, and feisty. Some of them are just never going to be happy with what you do, even if you've worked a miracle on a deal. You can't be beaten down by those people, or just quit the relationship, because it would mean closing a door on yourself and losing a great opportunity to do business together.

Much depends on how you approach such people—whether you can make them receptive to what you want to say. Before the business at hand is even mentioned, try saying something that will *release tension,* to get them thinking the way you are thinking. For example, you might flatter those people by giving them the credit for what you know you have accomplished. You did it, you might tell them; it was your great meeting or accomplishments or whatever that made things go so well. (You are being honest doing this, because ultimately, they deserve credit for it anyway.)

Don't be intimidated by reputation.

Again, find ways to win people over to your side.

You are going in for an interview for a very important job in a firm that is known to be difficult about hiring people. You can ease the tension and impress the people who interview you by showing them that you have done your research on the company and that you consider the prospect of being associated with them a great privilege.

Use this type of approach whenever you find yourself faced with a difficult person or situation, and you are in need of hearing a yes.

WHAT HAVE YOU GOT TO LOSE?

For my friend Melville Shavelson, a screenwriter, director, producer and, most recently, coauthor with Bob Hope of Hope's best-seller, *Don't Shoot, It's Only Me,* that receptive approach to life's experiences was what launched his career:

I had just graduated from a prestigious Ivy League school—Cornell University—and went to find work in New York, New York, because, if you can make it there, you'll make it anywhere. Sinatra hadn't even sung that song yet, because the year was 1937, but I was young enough to believe it.

I hit the jackpot. Almost immediately I was writing two network radio shows at the same time—We, the People, and something called The Bicycle Party, for the Bicycle Manufacturers of America, in a day when a bicycle was transportation, not a way of losing weight.

I was cocky, happy, living in an apartment in Greenwich Village, and convinced that life would go on like this forever.

Then I had a visit from Santa Claus. On December twenty-fourth The Bicycle Party was canceled, and I was simultaneously informed that We, the People, all of them, could get along without me. Sometimes it's not one door that closes, but two or three—and right on your fingers.

I still can't stand Christmas carols.

With the rent to pay and the small problem of eating, I searched frantically for work. I finally got a job with a

Broadway press agent, Milt Josefsberg, for the magnificent salary of thirteen dollars a week.

The only reason I took the work, in addition to a strong urge to avoid malnutrition, was that Milt had told me he knew a struggling young comic then playing vaudeville at Loew's State Theater, who was looking for writers for his very first radio show. I went to Loew's to see him, and was singularly unimpressed. Too glib, too sharp, the kid was due for a quick exit.

Milt agreed, but insisted it didn't matter because the fellow had a contract to do the radio show for thirteen weeks, practically a lifetime, before he could be canceled. What did we have to lose by writing a script for him on "speculation"? I had never heard that word before until Milt explained it meant "for free," then I realized I had heard it quite often. I rebelled for a while, but finally sat down with Milt and we wrote twenty pages of jokes, after which Milt informed me we were now partners. And he was giving up his business.

I was flattered until I realized I had gone from being a salaried employee to half owner of nothing in only two weeks. Progress.

Two days later we got a phone call from the young comic. He had read our jokes and wanted us to meet him at the Hampshire House to discuss salary.

He had said the magic word. I immediately decided he was the greatest comedian in the world. We raced over. When we arrived, breathing hard, at his hotel room, he offered each of us the magnificent sum of one hundred dollars a week and a ticket to a place called Hollywood. I had never been west of Lindy's Delicatessen, but I accepted. So did Milt, although he had a fear of Indians.

By the way, have I mentioned the struggling young

comic's name? Leslie Townes Hope, sometimes known as
"Bob."
   The show lasted more than thirteen weeks.

Had Shavelson closed the door on himself by not taking that thirteen-dollar-a-week job with the press agent; had he quit when he thought that young comic was "due for a quick exit"—the door to the biggest opportunity in his career would never have opened.

DON'T LET A NEGATIVE ATTITUDE BE AN OBSTACLE.

Use television producer Eve Silverman's wonderfully down-to-earth approach in trying anything. It will open a door every time:

> *My story is about when I was first starting out, looking for my first job. I knew I wanted to be a producer, but I had no idea how many different meanings there were to the word* producer—*it could have meant doing hundreds and hundreds of different things.*
>
> *A woman from an advertising agency was looking for an assistant producer and I decided this was the job I had to have. It was probably doing toilet-paper commercials, but I wanted to work in an agency and I*

wanted to work for her. I knew there were many other women competing for the job because she asked us all to come to a class she was teaching. But I was an Ivy League graduate and full of myself; despite the competition I was very confident that I was going to get this job. So when this woman called me to tell me that I did not get the job, I was flabbergasted. Looking back, it never really occurred to me that sometimes people have other reasons besides ability as to why they don't hire people, that maybe I posed some sort of threat to her or something like that, but anyway, I was just devastated.

It happened that the next day I went to a film seminar and one of the speakers was a very successful woman in film. I was so impressed with her that I went up to her after the seminar and said, "I'll work for you for free. I just want to learn how you do what you do; it sounds so incredible."

"That's wonderful!" she said. "You can read and evaluate two books for me and that will let me see if you'd be right for the job. Come to my office today and pick them up. I would like story reports on my desk tomorrow morning."

Well, I went to her office and she gave me two six-hundred-page manuscripts. I stayed up all night reading and I wrote up reports as best as I could and dropped them off, bleary-eyed, the next morning.

The next day the woman called me and said, "You're hired. Anyone who would be idiot enough to do this probably has a future in this business."

That was my first job, at Highgate Pictures. That's where I learned how to do what I'm doing now. I started as a secretary, and eventually started producing all their after-school specials, and then I started my own *company, doing my own television after-school specials and movies.*

I might add that after that first rejection, I also learned about networking—women helping other women. Had I been the one turning down a college graduate, for whatever reason, I certainly would have given that person seven hundred names of other people to call, which I do as a practice now. It's important to do that.

THERE'S NOTHING WRONG WITH A LITTLE IGNORANCE.

When I was sixteen and eager to find summer work, I wrote letter after letter to every possible source I could think of, including the Cunard Lines. Little did I imagine that my age and 5' 4" height would hold me back from a job with them—to say nothing of the fact that I was not a member of the Teamsters union! The person who read my letter at Cunard must have had quite a laugh—an inquiry from a young boy in Brooklyn willing to do anything from scrubbing decks to washing dishes in order to see the world—but that inclination to try things once has served me well in life, providing as much fun as success.

At one point in my career, when I was involved with popular music and recording, managing an orchestra and a well-known singer, I got the idea of producing a series of children's stories and songs on record with well-known personalities. I'd be contacting these people out of the blue, but it seemed to me worth a try because no matter how big a star might be, the idea of their doing something fun for children made the project unusually appealing.

Maybe it was because I had young children of my own then, but it turned out my hunch was right and a great number of celebrities agreed to do the narrations—Greer Garson, Ed McMahon, Ralph Bellamy, Bill Stern, the sportscaster, and many, many others. Even when I was turned down I had lots of fun, because more often than not, there I'd be speaking directly on the telephone to one of the top stars of the day. Cary Grant and I chatted for about half an hour about the project. He told me he loved the idea and wished he could do it but he was just too busy; and he wished me all kinds of good luck. It was terrific talking to him.

Jack Benny called. I thought my secretary was kidding when she announced who it was on the phone, but sure enough, there was Jack himself telling me that he would love to do bedtime stories for children and what a great idea it was, but he was overcommitted at the time and he, too, wished me the best of luck. Before the day was over, I received another telephone call, from Greer Garson, one of my favorite stars. When I'd first contacted her, she had written back saying she just couldn't do a recording because of her schedule. Since then, she explained, her mother had passed away and one of her last wishes had been for Greer to do the children's record album for me. She was calling to make the arrangements.

"Greer," I said, somewhat in shock, "I am absolutely delighted about this, but I just want you to know that I cannot afford to fly you in from California, and all I can manage to pay is five hundred dollars for your services."

"Artie," she responded, "the money is unimportant. I have an apartment at the Hampshire House and I'll stay there. You just get me the script and I will come in."

Well, I sat right down and wrote the script and sent it on to her, and sure enough she came in as promised and did the album and it turned out to be a wonderful recording.

On the day we finished working in the studio, I gave her a gold charm for a charm bracelet, in the form of a record, saying *Thank you* on it, and I asked her if she'd let me take her out to dinner to celebrate. She agreed. That evening I picked her up at the Hampshire House and off we went to the best restaurant I could think of, only to find that it was absolutely jammed. Foolishly I had not made a reservation, and there were no tables. As I stood there with Greer Garson, embarrassed as can be and wondering what to do, the captain came running over to us saying, "Oh, just a moment, just a moment," and there was a whole commotion as they brought out a special table for us and set it up right in the middle of the restaurant.

Greer Garson told me how impressed she was that they knew me so well and treated me so nicely, but of course they couldn't have cared less about me. They just wanted to show Greer Garson off to their patrons. Greer knew that, too, I'm sure, but she was such a lady about the whole situation, she never once gave the impression that the table became available because of who she was rather than who I wasn't.

Meeting so nice a person as Greer Garson and becoming friends with her certainly would not have happened if I had not had the nerve to go ahead and contact her, as I did with so many other celebrities.

Try anything. Chances are you will have a lot of fun in the process of opening doors, and eventually luck will come your way.

10

SEIZE SERENDIPITY

*"The secret of success in life is for a man to be ready for
his opportunity when it comes."*
BENJAMIN DISRAELI (1804–1881),
English statesman and author

*"Great opportunities come to all, but many do
not know they have met them."*
ALBERT ELIJAH DUNNING (1844–1923),
American editor

The perfect door may be in front of you, but you
must be prepared to recognize it.

KEEP YOUR EYES OPEN FOR SERENDIPITY.

Show business is filled with great stories of being at
the right place at the right time.

For Milton Berle, one of the great comedians of
all time, serendipity was waiting in a train station,
although he did not recognize it for what it was.
Fortunately, his mother was along, and she knew a
rare opportunity when she saw one. Milton Berle
describes what happened:

In the early days of vaudeville, when you played the small-time circuits, you never turned any booking down. Vaudeville engagements were hard to come by, and when I lost a split week in Elmira, New York, when the theater had to close for repairs because of a fire, it seemed like a very big door had slammed shut on me.

Not that my future was really bleak, it only seemed bleak. If the rug was pulled out from under a vaudevillian for even one night, you felt like it was the end of the world, like your career was over.

My mother suggested we stop over in Newburgh, New York, on our way home, to catch a vaudeville show there. She thought it might cheer me up, and also, being a very practical lady, she figured I might pick up a pointer or two, even a joke or two to use in my own act.

Arriving in Newburgh two hours before the show, we sat in the railroad station. My mother was drinking coffee, and I was eating oranges. My diet in those days consisted pretty much of oranges; cheap and easy to eat.

A half hour after our arrival there was a hubbub in the railroad station. Moran and Mack, the comedy stars of the bill in Newburgh, were arguing and shouting at each other over a personal matter. They were ready to quit the engagement.

They were followed into the station a moment later by the theater owner in Newburgh. He pleaded with the headliners to return to the theater and do the show. Charlie Mack refused. Not only did Mack not want to work with Moran, he didn't want to be in the same city, the same country, or on the same planet.

My mother overheard the whole conversation and within thirty seconds she had convinced the theater owner she had a great replacement for the headliners . . .

me. Besides that, Mom then held the theater owner up for
another thirty bucks.

I took over the Moran and Mack spot and wowed
them. The theater owner's report to the booker of the
entire circuit was a glowing review. A week later I was
booked on a bigger circuit. I kept working and polishing
my act until the GIANT door opened for me and there
was the big time . . . the Palace Theater on Broadway.
P.S. If opportunity doesn't knock . . . build a door.

DON'T LET THE RIGHT TIME PASS YOU BY.

Show-biz mothers are not the only ones with a
talent for recognizing serendipity for their children.
Andrea Richman Golden, a dentist whose practice
is on the north shore of Long Island, had been
divorced for a year when her mother saw serendipity spring up from the past. In her daughter's
words:

I had been divorced for about a year when one day, my
mother said to me, "I hear that Alan Golden has also
gone through a divorce."

You would have to have some background to know
what this news meant to me. I had known Alan since the
time I was a baby. Alan's family lived across the street
and he became my brother's best friend. Up until I was

twelve I didn't even know Alan existed, but from then on through my teens, I had a secret crush on him. He came to the house all the time and we would talk for hours. I knew that he liked me, too, but because of our age difference (he was six years older than I was), we never dated.

When I was about eighteen years old, Alan got married, and my heart sank. And by the time I was twenty-one, I had married someone else.

So here we were, as my mother pointed out, both of us divorced—both of us in the same situation. Six years apart in age suddenly did not seem like such a big difference.

I did not hesitate picking up the phone to call him, and from our first date we felt totally comfortable together, just like old times. Alan proposed to me immediately, but I told him I thought we should wait and see if we did really get along—even so, I had no doubts. Right from the beginning we both knew it was meant to be, and a few months later I decided it was perfect, and in the spring we got married.

If I had married Alan from the beginning, I don't know if the relationship would have worked, because I was going to dental school and that put a lot of stress on my marriage. Timing was very important, but it's funny, because after just the first phone call I knew that everything was going to work out. I told a friend of mine after seeing Alan for the first time again that it had been a very special day for me and I knew this was going to be it.

If my mother had not told me about Alan's availability, if I had dismissed it or waited or decided to just forget about it, my new beginning might never have come about. We have been married over seven years, we have a new baby, and it still feels like we're on our honeymoon.

George Lang, one of the great restaurateurs of the world and owner of the Café des Artistes restaurant in New York City, sums up the nature of serendipity:

> *In my opinion the key to being able to take advantage of opportunities is being ready for them! If not today, then tomorrow; if not this chance, then the next one will give you the opportunity and the vehicle to do at least part of the task that you are supposed to do on this Earth—as long as you are ready for it.*

PUT YOURSELF IN THE VICINITY OF YOUR DREAMS.

This is what the highly successful film and television producer and writer Edgar Scherick did, so that he was well prepared for seizing serendipity when it came along:

> *I had been working at an advertising agency in New York for about six years after completing Army service and college, and a job opened up at CBS that was my life's ideal—director of sports. All my life I had loved sports. I had written sports for my high school and college paper. My experience with television and sports at the agency certainly qualified me for the CBS job. I knew the business from stem to stern.*
>
> *An interview was arranged with Sig Mickelson, who*

was in charge of news at CBS and who also had responsibility for sports. His assistant, Elmer Lower, attended the meeting as well.

At the time, the CBS Sports Department was an unsophisticated affair, as TV sports was far from the giant industry it is today. CBS sports was not well run, in my opinion, and I really thought I could do a much better job than the incumbent personnel. I was not bashful in telling this to Mickelson and Lower. What I failed to perceive was that they were not interested in someone who was going to uproot things in an effort to make them better. They wanted someone who was not going to rock the boat. They had the wrong fellow in me. I loved the idea of the job and could not wait to start making things hum around CBS.

As you may suspect, I did not get the job despite the fact that I was eminently qualified by dint of my experience. Instead it went to a person from outside the television industry, the son of an illustrious sports executive.

I thought I was going to die. That job at that time was the most important thing in the world to me. I found myself unable to sleep. I awoke every morning for three weeks at four A.M., and to try to tire myself I donned my jogging clothes and ran the deserted streets on the East Side of Manhattan.

Finally the disappointment wore off and I actually joined CBS in the sports sales area, working closely with the new director of sports. We became good friends. It wasn't his fault I hadn't got the job I truly wanted, the job he had.

I was at CBS for about six months when I saw an opportunity for myself in a sports series that CBS was canceling—televising the Big Ten basketball games. I approached the commissioner of the conference and told *him that I could keep his conference on the air if he assigned to me the rights to televise his games. He did. I quit CBS, and that was the beginning of my life as an independent entrepreneur. Sig Mickelson and Elmer Lower provided me, at the same time, with the biggest disappointment of my life and my greatest opportunity.*

MEETING NEW PEOPLE

Increase your chances of meeting new people; of being at the right place at the right time:

Pursue your areas of interest.

Activities that give *you* special pleasure—and that includes your favorite sport, hobby, cultural activity, and so on—are a powerful resource in helping you meet new people who share those interests.

If your sport is tennis, for example, and you love to play the game, don't just stop there. Join a tennis club, get to tennis events, browse in the tennis area of sporting-goods stores, being prepared to open up a conversation on the subject of tennis with other customers you find attractive.

111

Expand your interests.

Consider volunteer work for the local hospital, park, school, et cetera. Not only will you feel good about contributing something of real value to a good cause, but you will certainly develop new friendships.

Join or establish a group that attracts like-minded people.

Participate in a reading group or an informal writers' workshop. Take a night class. Take a cooking class. Join the local birding club! Pitch in to work for the environment, the local park, or another area that concerns you. Learn more about the political process on a local level.

Whatever your "community of interest," put yourself where you will meet other people. Look for ways to stand out. Women love to see men pursue activities such as cooking, and gardening, just as men are drawn to women who enjoy home repair, working out with weights, computer science, and so on.

Pursue these endeavors with the idea of enjoying yourself and making new friends, and who knows, you may just open the door to meeting someone special.

ONE DOOR CLOSES, ANOTHER DOOR OPENS

There are many ways of making new doors open for yourself. One of them is being ready for that quirky situation known as serendipity—knowing an opportunity when it comes along, and seizing it.

11

BUILD A DOOR

"I have become my own version of an optimist. If I can't make it through one door, I'll go through another door—or I'll make a door. Something terrific will come no matter how dark the present."
JOAN RIVERS (b. 1933),
Comedienne

"If opportunity doesn't knock ... build a door."
MILTON BERLE (b. 1908),
Comic/Entertainer

THERE ARE NO GUARANTEES IN LIFE.

Mary Kay Ash, the creator of Mary Kay Cosmetics, offers a wonderful example of building a door, but not before tragedy was to challenge her dream. Her story proves that there are no guarantees in life and that sometimes you must be willing to take a chance.

In 1963, after working in direct sales for twenty-five years, with two companies, I retired for a whole month. I knew that retirement was not for me, and I was very restless. I was very concerned about the plight of women in the early 1960s—talented, capable women I'd met through work who simply did not have an opportunity to break the glass ceiling and enter the top ranks of business. I knew that if given the opportunity, these women could do anything in this world they wanted to do, but that opportunity was simply not available to them at that time.

Addressing my concerns, I sat down with the intention of writing a book that would help other women through some of the obstacles that I had overcome. I really didn't know how to write a book, but I began by simply putting on a legal-size pad all of the good things that the two companies I had worked for had done.

After a couple of weeks I took a second legal-size pad and began writing down the problems we had encountered, and there were many. When I had finished this exercise, I realized I had inadvertently put on paper a marketing plan that would, indeed, give women the opportunity I wanted them to have. I thought, Wouldn't it be great if somebody did this instead of just wrote about it? It was from that idea that Mary Kay Cosmetics was born. My objective was simply to help women. Of course I hoped the business would pay its way and we would make a living, but of that I really wasn't sure.

My husband was to handle the administrative end of the business, since that was his area of expertise, and I would handle the motivational and recruiting portion of our new company. One month to the day before we were to open our doors, with every penny we had in the world spent or committed, my husband died at the breakfast table of a heart attack. Suddenly I had only half a company, for I knew nothing of the administrative end.

For me the phrase goes, "When God closes a door, He always opens a window," and it came in the form of my twenty-year-old son. I didn't know if Richard could fulfill the obligations he had to undertake. He had two years of marketing at North Texas University, but no experience. It was traumatic. Little did I know that just five short years later that young man would be recognized as one of the financial geniuses of our nation, and is still well known for his business acumen today.

At that point in my life I questioned God's judgment, but as always, He knew best. We began with a mere five-thousand-dollar investment, at that time my whole life savings, and today our company is approaching the billion-dollar mark in retail sales with over 220,000 consultants in fourteen countries around the world.

"Find a need and fill it—but don't resort to gimmicks! If you fill a real need, you'll have a loyal following."
ADRIEN ARPEL,
Founder of her own multimillion-dollar cosmetics company

USE THE CLOSED DOOR AS YOUR INSPIRATION TO ACCOMPLISH MORE THAN YOU EVER THOUGHT YOU COULD.

When I described this book to my good friend Godfrey Isaac, a leading Los Angeles attorney, he responded immediately by telling me he'd be happy to contact his brother, Ted, who had a powerful story about one door closing, another door opening.

Diagnosed with emphysema at age forty-one, Ted Isaac was told by doctors he'd be lucky to live another five years—later he found out they had actually given him less than a year. The door to the future (*any* future) had slammed shut, leaving Isaac with the challenge of finding some way to support his family after he was gone—his wife and children aged three, four, and five.

One night very late in my hospital bed, I sat up and calculated that when I died in five years, I would have to have a million dollars to cover my children's future. This was an unimaginable sum to a man earning fifteen thousand dollars a year, but that's what I would need. The hospital discharged me just after the new year—out I went back into the world, but with a terminal diagnosis. As time and I stumbled on, I learned an obvious lesson: You can't save a million dollars in five years—not on fifteen thousand a year; not in a hundred years. I had to do better. I started a moonlight business, After Hours Advertising. It doubled my income, but by then I had only four years to live. I'd still never save a million dollars in that short time.

Then I had a brainstorm. My wife received money-saving coupons for store products in the mail—manufacturers sent out billions of these cents-off coupons every year by direct mail. I would distribute them in a new way, printing them on a single sheet and selling them as a supplement to the Sunday newspapers. It would save the advertisers millions of dollars in direct mail costs, and maybe it would make a million dollars for me.

For two years I struggled with various ways to print and distribute coupons in newspapers, until finally my big break came. One sticky August afternoon the promotion manager of a major corporation called to ask, "Ted, is it reasonable for you to distribute thirty-five million coupons for us next January?" Up to then I'd never distributed a million anything.

I said, "No, it's not. But let me try." Thirty-five million coupons meant a $350,000 order for me, $250,000 in my pocket if I succeeded; a million-dollar bankruptcy if I didn't. I had to do it, and I did. Three months later I called them back to say, "I'm ready to go." Ninety days later I had $250,000 in the bank and I'd launched a new industry. Later that year, on December twenty-third, five years after my sleepless night in the hospital, I signed a contract to sell my new coupon business for over a million dollars—the money for my children's future.

By then I had discovered that even doctors can make mistakes. They had diagnosed my illness incorrectly, but for that I have to thank them. If it were not for receiving a diagnosis of terminal illness, I'd still be sitting behind a middle-management desk, pulling down a middle-management salary.

I did not die, nor do I expect to die soon. My desperation business is a billion-dollar industry. I enjoy the future I never expected to have in a house perched high above beautiful Kaneohe Bay, Hawaii.

I learned a lesson that long-ago night in the hospital: Don't wait for a death sentence to explode into action. Your future becomes what you make it.

WORK, WORK, WORK—BUT ALWAYS WITH A WINNING ATTITUDE.

If you have been in a field for ten to fifteen years and you have a good track record, contacts, and credibility, consider free-lancing in your field.

My good friend Leonore Fleischer is a perfect example of what it takes to work for yourself. She's one of those people who, on first meeting, you just know will never let a door close on themselves without turning it into something terrific. She writes weekly columns for *New York* magazine and *Publishers Weekly,* writes novels, and does adaptations of movies under a pseudonym.

Leonore's hardworking attitude is proof that *when you step out and take a chance, chances are you are ready for it:*

> All my life I have worked. I worked after school hours in junior high and in high school, wrapping packages at the Fordham Road Alexander's. When I was graduated from Bronx Science High School at sixteen, I went to work full time. (College was where you went at night, and it was free.) I was the child of a working-class family in the Depression, when there was no work. A steady job was viewed by my family as the only form of security you could clutch to, and on the few occasions that I left a job on a Friday, it was to start a new one on Monday.
>
> When I was thirty-six years old, a door closed with

divorce. What I took with me out of my marriage was a four-year-old child, no alimony, no child support. At that time I was a mass-market-paperback editor earning exactly enough, after taxes were taken out of my check, to pay a child-care person five days a week. There wasn't a cent left over for rent, food, utilities, or any other luxury of life.

I knew I'd have to work two jobs. If I were Margaret Rudkin, I might have baked cookies and become Pepperidge Farm. If I were a better typist, I'd have typed envelopes at a couple of dollars per hundred. The only skill I had was that I could string a couple of words together. I began free-lance writing, no job too small. I wrote press releases, catalog copy, flap copy—twenty-five dollars here; fifty there; it added up. I worked all day at my editing job, and all night every night and weekends. I caught up with my rent and avoided eviction (I'd already received the notice). The free-lance work became better. I reviewed the occasional book for Life magazine or the World, Journal, or Tribune. I began writing paperback novelizations of film scripts, first for a fifteen-hundred-dollar flat fee, then for three thousand plus a two percent royalty, gradually for a lot more.

I left my full-time job for another, on a struggling national magazine. The pay was better, even if the outlook for the publication was risky. I kept on writing in the evenings—all evening, every evening; all weekend, every weekend—supplementing my paycheck. Then one day, it happened—the dreaded pink slip in the pay envelope. The whole office was closing down and for the first time since I was sixteen years old, I had no assured weekly income.

My security was gone; the door had closed. Another first: I was collecting unemployment insurance, standing on line one morning a week (no consolation that once Christopher Walken was standing on line behind me) to collect a hundred dollars. I was paralyzed. Where should I go to find a new job? I was so ashamed. Who would hire somebody that somebody else had fired?

New York magazine tried me out several weeks for the "Sales & Bargains" column, and I landed it. Within another week or so I had landed "Letter from New York" with The Washington Post. Both were flukes, good-luck accidents, but put together they were a weekly income that was the equivalent of a job. Now, suddenly a door opened and I looked into a different world. Suppose I didn't go back to working nine to five? Suppose I did the columns and the books, instead of the books and a job?

It occurred to me that perhaps the open door meant that I could be a serious person, working for myself, getting up early, meeting deadlines, not needing the crutch of a weekly paycheck from an unrewarding job. I went for it.

Twenty years later I'm still working free-lance. I use a computer and a fax machine. I can take breaks in the middle of the day to hug one or more of my cats; my son is married. I still work weekends, though. Somewhere, there's got to be another door. . . .

DON'T JUST DREAM ABOUT THE POSSIBILITIES FOR MAKING A NEW START. PLAN YOUR EXIT.

When you feel a door is closing, do as Sharon Mesmer did—give yourself that fair chance at something you would love to try but would otherwise have ignored:

By the age of twenty-five I'd been active in the Chicago literary community for six years—writing, publishing, reading my fiction and poetry in public, and coediting two magazines.

By twenty-six I had begun to feel as if I were spinning my wheels. It seemed the door had opened for me in Chicago about as far as it would go. I wanted to do more, learn more, be in direct contact with more writers, build a wider audience for my work.

Chicago was my hometown. It was a great city, full of family, friends, and inspiration, but I knew that New York was always the place to be for a writer. If I stayed in Chicago, it would be for sentimental reasons—or because I wasn't courageous enough to make the change I knew I had to make.

I applied and was accepted for admission into the Master of Fine Arts Program in Creative Writing at Brooklyn College. Through the program I was able to get an apartment, and a job teaching at the college. I was able to study with the poet Allen Ginsberg, one of my greatest literary influences, and through his recommendation I received a prestigious MacArthur Foundation Scholarship. As part of Brooklyn College's Summer Study in Europe program, I taught a creative writing class in Paris. Reading my work at the Nuyorican Poets Café on the Lower East Side, I was asked to appear in the season premiere of Alive from Off Center, *a highly acclaimed PBS series featuring poets, playwrights, and performance artists. A literary agent is interested in my work, giving me greater incentive than ever to work hard.*

123

None of these opportunities would have come along if I had stayed in Chicago. I followed my instincts in making a move, and although it was a gamble, it has definitely paid off.

LEAVING A JOB, LANDING A JOB

Keep your head and don't panic when a door appears to close.

If you find yourself in an office or industry that is temporarily foundering, undergoing an upheaval or a change in management, don't contemplate quitting because everyone else is talking about quitting or losing their job. The situation may appear bleak, but hard times do not automatically signal that your job will end, even if others around you are being let go.

Look your situation over carefully; put uncertainty into perspective.

Is your industry healthy? Even if the answer is negative, it is the company that is the employer, not the industry. A badly run company stands a greater chance than a well-run one of being affected by recession. Base your assessment on your own company's performance and your individual situation.

Is your particular region in a slump? Some regions of the country are more affected by a recession and job loss than others, despite what the news says about the recession being nationwide.

How directly do you contribute to the bottom line? If there were cutbacks, would your job be expendable? When times are tough, the farther one's work is from the customer, the greater the chances an employee has to lose out.

Tailor these and other questions you might have to your situation. Clarify whether a door is really closing before you make a move.

Never quit a job before you have a new one lined up.

Don't let your negative emotions get the better of you. You'll only make things worse than they are by getting angry and storming out. If you are miserable, make new plans and act on them.

Your value is a hundred times greater to a potential employer when you are working for someone else.

You are in a much better bargaining position if you are neither in a rush to be hired nor instantly attainable. "I have a good job, but I am looking for a change"—that's so much better than having to say you are unemployed.

If you have been given notice and told you will be let go in four weeks or in a given length of time: stay put.

Do everything you can to find something else. Your staying on may be "dead time" to your company, but you're still on the payroll with a desk and a phone and letterhead stationery at your disposal, and that interim period can be invaluable in making the move from your current position into something better.

Look for ways to harness your talents in new areas.

If your particular situation really *is* in trouble, again, don't panic. Think *career,* not *company.* Ingenuity can provide you with a golden opportunity to move ahead. If there really is trouble in your industry—banking, real estate, et cetera—don't set your sights on competing for the same kind of job in a failing marketplace. Choose new areas of work in related fields where your skills can be turned into assets.

Network.

It's said that nearly two thirds of new jobs are found through contacts built up over one's career. Use that network. One contact leads to another—in a sense, that's what life is all about. Be willing to ask for favors, at the same time be willing to perform them. And don't be afraid to reach out for advice and emotional support among peers and colleagues. It is one of the most effective ways to keep morale up when you are looking for a job—and to keep momentum going.

Carefully research your market and prospective employer.

Why would you be especially valuable to this or that particular company?

Find that "extra something" in your background and experience that can will give you an edge on the competition.

Prepare your resume or interview to show why you would bring something to the job and company that someone else may not be able to do. For example, your competition for the job may be just as well-educated as you are and have just as many work experiences, but you may be a good accountant, know how to set up computer programs, know something about law that the next person cannot offer.

Sell yourself to the person you would want to work for, not to the personnel department.

Determine your priorities. I

The top-rung position or that job with a giant conglomerate may not be right for you. If it's not, *be willing to downshift.*

While not selling yourself short, look for a job that first and foremost shows real potential for harnessing your skills and aspirations, even if that means trading down. Taking a more satisfying job at a lower level may very well be a terrific move for you if it gives you the time you have always wanted to spend with your family, or pursuing a hobby, or traveling.

Many people, including top executives, have discovered they enjoy getting off the fast track and settling for smaller incomes than they had pursued previously. If this approach sounds appealing, consider tailoring your managerial skills to temporary work, three days a week, for example—trading time for freedom.

Trade up, if that's your goal. When a door closes, have the confidence to think big—to stand up and say, "This is what I want to do." Go after it.

Broadcast, don't hide, your age and experience.

Package yourself effectively. Don't let inexperience (or too much experience) stand in your way. Keep after what you want to do, make contacts every day, and eventually the door will open. You probably know more people than you think, in many diverse walks of life. Use your ingenuity and creativity to determine how best you can present your objectives to friends and associates, for assistance and possibly a break in reaching your objectives. You'd do the same for them.

Challenge conventional wisdom when looking for a job.

Don't be afraid to debunk standard procedures or ways of thinking if they do not work for you. There is no one tried-and-true way of doing anything. When challenged, conventional wisdom often crumbles, as the following six examples show:

1. Conventional Wisdom: The holiday season is the worst time to look for a job.

This is similar to the mistaken idea that the last place to look for work is the company that's laying people off—it's not always true. For some people holidays turn out to be the best time to find new work. The competition is low; the boss, unless he or she is a retailer, is usually available and receptive to talk. *Don't stop the momentum of looking for work just because the time of year or some other factor seems to intrude.*

2. Conventional Wisdom: A big company is the best place to find work.

Stories abound of young men and women who attend the best colleges in the country, graduate at the top of their class, go out to look for employment in the field they trained for—law, for example—and, due to the economy or some other unforeseen circumstance, cannot land a job.

If you are such a graduate, do a little more introspection before you jump into the job search. Take a step back and consider what path is right for you. Avoid becoming "trapped" in large firms and expensive life-styles, where someplace else you might have a satisfying career.

In times when jobs in the big firms are scarce, you will do much better looking for work in the public sector, in small firms, and in firms outside of big cities. Use your ingenuity.

3. Conventional Wisdom: Look for the best-paying job around because job security no longer exists.

No matter what you hear, job security will always be tied to performance. Those who love what they are doing and do it well are usually the last to go. Let job satisfaction be your guiding principle.

4. Conventional Wisdom: If you are over fifty, you'll have a hard time finding work.

Experience, not age, counts today in the job market. Networking groups such as Forty Plus can help middle-aged unemployed executives and job seekers strengthen their resumes and explore new avenues for work.

Seasoned experience can open possibilities for an advisory position, or temporary work.

Perhaps skills can be reapplied to an entirely new area of employment, in a whole new location. A new environment and new surroundings are just what some people need to direct new careers to new success.

5. Conventional Wisdom: Entrepreneurship only succeeds for those who are under forty.

When you lose a job, it may be a great time for you to start a business of your own, particularly if you are in or around your fifties. A firing blasts many executives out of their rut. No matter what you are, be willing to take a chance. You may be well suited for self-employment or starting your own business.

6. Conventional Wisdom: Temporary work has no benefits, it ties up your time, and it gets you nowhere.

In fact, the opposite proves true. "Temp work" may be the best way to give you direction and formulate plans for the future.

Many temps find their niche in a particular assignment and pursue permanent jobs with the firm; others opt for their own freedom, pursuing side interests of their own.

It takes flexibility, patience, and a pleasant manner to take on this type of work, but it can provide time to evaluate the future or pursue dreams.

These are but a few examples of how conventional wisdom can be challenged to make way for new opportunities. Look, listen, and debunk. Don't let "standard procedures" defeat you.

You don't have to be a genius to think creatively about making new doors open; all it takes is ingenuity and common sense. Let the closed door lead you to a more original way of thinking.

> *"By the streets of 'by and by' one arrives*
> *at the house of 'never.' "*
> MIGUEL DE CERVANTES (1547–1616)

Don't just dream about the possibilities for making a new start. When a door closes, take that chance and go after something you always wanted to try but may have held back on. This may be your golden opportunity.

12

YOUR TURN TO CLOSE A DOOR?

"Truth is not only violated by falsehood; it may be equally outraged by silence."
HENRI FRÉDÉRIC AMIEL (1821–1881),
Swiss philosopher

Difficult as it may be, do not be afraid to close a door on someone else.

PUT YOURSELF FIRST.

Don't do it in a self-serving way, but use your self-respect as a source of courage to speak out and close a door. Keep an eye out for people who would take advantage of you. When you spot such people and the time comes that you must close the door on them, for your own sake, go ahead and do it.

Paul Nathan, longtime columnist for *Publishers Weekly* magazine and a good friend, learned the lesson of looking out for oneself the hard way:

I needed a second source of income and knew that Walt Disney was looking for a New York story editor, a job that involved finding material for movies and the weekly

Disney TV show. I knew I could do this job. Each week my column featured news of subsidiary rights sales that had been made for a wide variety of books, and I had many contacts throughout the book industry. The Disney Studio editor came East and interviewed me, and then contacted almost everyone I knew in publishing through my column to attest to my fitness for the post. I flew out to California to be sized up by Walt himself. Our interview lasted only a few minutes, but a little later I was informed that I was hired and I flew back East.

I discovered that locating suitable stories for Disney was not as easy as I had anticipated. When I turned up what I thought were good possibilities, my Disney boss shot them down. Of one exciting tale about mountaineering he said, "Ever since Walt made Third Man on the Mountain, he hasn't wanted to touch anything about mountain climbing."

Of another book I liked—a charming tale set in Ireland—he told me Walt had "soured on Irish backgrounds" in the wake of Darby O'Gill and the Little People. And so on. With increasing desperation I sought out information on forthcoming books and combed publishers' libraries for titles published in the past—all to no avail.

On my second visit to the studio, some months after being hired, Walt wanted to review progress—or lack of it—to date. We met over lunch with my West Coast boss and about half a dozen other executives. Walt expressed disappointment that the pickings so far had been slim. He cited some movies from other studios that he would have liked to make. One was The Quiet Man, the very movie I had recommended. I reacted with surprise: "I thought that after Darby O'Gill you didn't want anything Irish."

"Where did you get that idea?" asked Walt.

I looked at my boss, expecting help, but no aid was to come from that quarter. "Well, I got the impression . . ." I floundered.

Then Walt mentioned a second picture of the type he was interested in—the very story I'd recommended about mountaineering. It had been optioned by another company. Again I flashed my boss a silent appeal for help, and I knew that my days with Disney were numbered. Shortly thereafter, I was out.

Today, in a similar situation, I would have never have been so passive defending myself. I would have said something to Disney like "I have memos from my boss here indicating you did not want such stories."

In other words, I would have closed the door on him! However, I was young and naive and I felt incapable of causing the embarrassment that would come from publicly exposing the guilty party.

STEP IN, SPEAK UP, AND BE READY TO CLOSE THE DOOR.

You may be dating someone for a while and seeing her three times a week. Suddenly she tells you she is going to be busy next week and can see you only once. That could be, but if it happens again and eventually that person tells you she can see you only once a week, you have every reason to think she may be seeing someone else or that the relationship has changed.

Find out what's going on. Discuss it. If there is someone else in the picture, think carefully about whether it is worth trying to put the relationship back where you want it, or better to end it. Let your intuition be your guide.

DON'T BE AFRAID OF A CONFRONTATION.

If you see that people you love are hurting themselves or someone else by their actions, confront them with what you see. Even if it means risking friendship or love, if it helps them close the door on what they are doing, it is worth the risk.

I know a widower in his early seventies who, for a year after his wife died, would with increasing frequency pour himself a drink. His two grown daughters continued to visit him frequently as they had always done when both parents were alive, but their father became more and more difficult as he turned to liquor—staying at home by himself, ignoring his friends, giving up his outside responsibilities, forgetting to pay his bills.

Over and over his daughters pleaded with him to

stop drinking, but it had no effect. One day they told him outright, "Dad, we love you so much when you are sober and we'll always love you no matter what, but we just can't get together with you when you are drunk."

They were willing to risk closing the door on their own father, hoping it would jolt him into pulling himself together and stop him from feeling sorry for himself. Six months went by before he called them to get together, but when he did, they heard the proud voice of a sober man on the other end of the phone. To this day he has not had another drink—and he's even found himself an outside job that he truly loves doing: hand-delivering packages to his daughter's clients around town. It gets him out of the house and downtown, he meets lots of interesting people—and he does a great public-relations job for her!

In another situation one parent cared so much for his eighteen-year-old son's welfare that he actually turned him in to the police when he found a bag of marijuana the boy had left on the front seat of the car.

"It was the toughest decision of my life, but I did it for his own good," said his father, describing how he drove his college-dropout son to the local police station, where he was booked on possession of drugs and kept in jail overnight. Pleading no contest, the boy was ordered to undergo drug counseling and if he managed to stay out of trouble for a year, the case would be erased from the books.

This act of moral courage turned out to be the best thing that the father ever did for his son, who "grew up," returned to college, and did so well he made dean's list. Ultimately, the whole experience brought the two of them closer together. "I can honestly say there's no animosity between us," the father explains. "I feel I did the right thing and my son agrees with me. We've both decided to put it all behind us and look to the future."

Do not be afraid to close a door on someone else. You may be the one person in someone's life who sees the truth of their situation—that the way they are handling themselves is bad for them, and for others. Closing a door on injustice, deceit, or harassment takes great courage and may even bring dire consequences, but the truth provides peace of mind.

13

MIRACLES OUT OF MISHAPS

"Stars may be seen from the bottom of a deep well, when they cannot be discerned from the top of a mountain. So are many things learned in adversity which the prosperous man dreams not of."
CHARLES HADDON SPURGEON (1834–1892),
English clergyman

"We are always in the forge or on the anvil; by trials God is shaping us for higher things."
HENRY WARD BEECHER (1813–1887),
American clergyman

THE DARKEST MOMENTS CAN TURN OUT TO THE GOOD.

Hilde Serlin, my son Richard's mother-in-law, provides the following story of how a dramatic, near-miss fall introduced her to a very special person in her life.

When my brother and I lived in New York City, we would occasionally meet after work at his sixth-floor studio on East Fifty-seventh Street, and from there go out to dinner together. One evening I left the studio a little ahead of him. I pushed the button for the elevator, and when it arrived at the sixth floor, I opened the door, stepped in without thinking, and fell into an empty shaftway, six floors deep.

*My brother and his partner, who had been just behind
me, ran down to the main floor and somehow managed to
open the door and call the police. An ambulance arrived.
Having gotten the call that a woman had fallen down an
elevator shaft, they were prepared for me to be DOA—
dead on arrival. But I wasn't dead. Somehow, on the way
down I had grabbed the center cable and because it was
the middle of winter and I had on thick gloves and a
heavy fur coat, my life was saved. I landed on top of the
elevator with nothing more than a few bruises and some
burns on my arm from sliding down that cable. They
took me to the hospital and once I was checked over, I
signed myself out.*

*I thought that was the end of my experience, but soon
after the accident I heard from the doctor who had been
in the ambulance with me. He wanted to know how I was
doing, and he asked me out for a date. That was the
beginning of how the attending physician in the ambulance became my future husband.*

GOOD SELDOM COMES BY MISTAKE.

The recovery time after a physical injury often brings
a unique kind of introspection—and a chance for
self-discovery. Melvyn I. Kinder—clinical psychologist and author of such best-selling books as *Smart
Women/Foolish Choices; Women Men Love,
Women Men Leave;* and *Going Nowhere Fast*—
describes how an accident in his childhood left such

an impression on him, it ultimately opened the door to his career as a writer.

When I was eleven years old, I challenged the girl next door to a bicycle race and we went speeding down our peaceful residential street. I was riding in the middle of the street, cutting down the curves, when all of a sudden a car appeared and hit me head-on. According to witnesses I flew twenty feet in the air and landed on the curb. I was unconscious for about five minutes, woke up, and saw about five inches of jagged white thigh bone sticking through my pant leg.

Needless to say, I was in shock. I thought I would never walk again, or at least that I would lose my leg. I was in the hospital for three months; they saved my leg and sent me home in a full body cast from chest to toes. For the next six months I had to lie in bed, and then for another six months after that I was put in another cast that enabled me to walk with crutches, but just barely. At first I was depressed and ashamed about my accident. I secretly believed that what had happened was a confirmation that something was wrong with me, that other kids didn't screw up like that. I was a "cripple" and a burden to my parents.

When my fifth-grade classmates came to visit me, I told my mother to tell them I was asleep. I was too embarrassed to let them see me lying there in such a helpless state. Once a week my teacher, Mrs. Gray, would come by to give me assignments and pick up my homework.

In time I had no more visitors and I retreated into another world, one which totally enveloped me—the world of reading, of literature, of history. I no longer needed any outside stimulation, nor did I mourn the loss of physical activity or social activity. Every other day I begged my mother to go to various libraries and pick up books for me. I became friendly with the librarians over the phone. A new reality opened up for me. There was nothing out there in the "real world" that could match the Greeks battling on the plains of Marathon, Sir Galahad questing after the Holy Grail, Lancelot and his fellow knights reaffirming their manhood with one exploit after another, heroic submarine captains stalking dreaded U-boats, and, yes, even football heroes crashing through opposing linemen—Jim Thorpe, Red Grange, giants, exemplars of courage. The fact that my muscular and fast young body went soft never bothered me. As the weeks of my recovery turned into months, I became an insatiable reader.

When I finally got into college, my love for reading and the pursuit of knowledge paved the way for outstanding academic accomplishments and success due entirely to the "door" that had opened to me as a young boy.

FATE IS WHAT YOU MAKE OF IT.

Katherine Dunn is another author who "ran afoul of the law," as Melvyn Kinder described it. Her novel *Geek Love* received excellent reviews when it was published by Alfred A. Knopf, Inc., and it was nominated for the National Book Award in 1989, establishing Katherine Dunn as one of the outstanding new novelists of our time. It was getting into trouble in her youth that became the raw material for her brilliant career as a writer.

There were a lot of slamming doors in this country the year John F. Kennedy was killed. I'd just turned eighteen and one of the coincidental results of the big-news assassination was the microscopic news that I got into a scrape and landed in jail. Emerging shortly thereafter with a felony conviction and two years of bench parole, I was terrified of ending up back behind bars. It seemed clear that I was at a crossroads. What was ordained and waiting for me was a life of pathetic petty crime. All poverty and stupidity. No glamour about it at all. I didn't trust myself to stay straight. I thought I needed a structure, a noncriminal equivalent to jail, to keep my head together artificially until I could learn to do it for myself.

Others my age were swept up in politics and philosophy. I was obsessed with my own future. I knew nothing about the escalation of fire in Vietnam and I decided to enlist in the military. But the Marines, the Air Force, the Navy, and the Army all turned me down. They didn't want anybody reeking of a fresh, hot felony conviction. I was pretty depressed until the alternative struck me. College. The state college wouldn't have cared if I were an ax murderer as long as I paid tuition and passed the classes. When that school opened its doors to me, it saved my life and prevented years of idiot, miniature criminality from afflicting the community.

Three years later I wrote my first novel, Attic, based on the involuntary research I'd done in jail.

SERIOUS ACCIDENTS INCREASE ONE'S APPRECIATION FOR THE SUFFERING OF OTHERS.

"I realized I wanted to do something good during my lifetime, by a warm hand and not a cold one," said Leslie Wexner after he survived a mountain-climbing accident in Colorado. Chairman of The Limited, Inc., one of the country's largest retail chains, with more than thirty-eight hundred stores including Henri Bendel, Victoria's Secret, and Lane Bryant, Wexner established a $250-million-dollar trust to support a broad range of organizations and programs in and around the state of Ohio.

LET OTHERS HEAR FROM YOU IN THEIR TIME OF SUFFERING.

The story of how Travis John nearly lost his life falling from a window is a powerful example of the good that comes from offering support to others in their time of need. Sally John describes the event and its aftermath:

We were down on the Jersey shore and I thought I had everything covered. The children were young—Travis was two and a half, Tommy was four, and Tammy was six—and I had taken a baby-sitter with me who had been carefully instructed not to let the kids out of her sight, especially Travis. He was the type of child who, if you told him something was hot, had to test it to make sure. In other words, a daredevil.

The baby-sitter had the boys. I had just bathed them and taken them to her and I said, "Don't take your eyes off these boys for a minute. I'm going up to get dressed and I'll be right back down."

It wasn't ten minutes later that I heard Tammy yell from the third floor, "Mommy, Mommy! Travis fell out the window!"

I ran outside expecting to see my child landed in the bushes, but the only window in the entire house that didn't have bushes or sand under it was the window Travis had fallen out of. He had bounced off the front fender of our car and onto the concrete sidewalk.

When I got to him, he was blue. Blood was coming out of his ear. He was unconscious; I picked him up instinctively, not even thinking of a broken neck or something; I just picked him up and held him. He felt like a dead fish, and I thought he was dead.

He wasn't, thank God; and we rushed him to the hospital. He had hemorrhaging on the brain, and they operated immediately to relieve the pressure and then he lapsed into a coma where his own body, and God, and Nature, had to take their time and decide when Travis was going to wake up, and come back to be Travis.

This is where we met Dr. Fred Epstein, the pediatric neurosurgeon who was referred to us by a doctor in

California. We consulted him, and he said he saw no signs of irreversible brain damage, just that Travis, in his own time, would wake up after his brain healed and be back as Travis, exactly as before.

It was a hard seventeen days of him being in a coma, but we were very lucky. Dr. Epstein gave us hope all along that he would be better, and in fact, he did recuperate fully.

Because my husband, Tommy John, was in the public eye, the entire country knew about the accident—the Yankees were in a pennant race and Tommy was one of the five starting pitchers. We heard from people in Rio de Janeiro, from Guam; we got letters from politicians and presidents, movie stars and doctors—all offering whatever they could to help. These were spontaneous gestures—for example, President Nixon's note was handwritten on a scrap of paper, off to the side as if he'd just read the news of our tragedy and had to write.

That meant a lot to us, hearing from people. It gave us more courage, more strength, to suffer through what we had to suffer. Because of that experience, when I hear stories of people suffering, I care a little more than I would have before Travis's accident, and I do what I can to show I care.

We learn something from every negative, every hurdle in life; we have to learn something by it. That's one of the things I learned from Travis's accident.

You must put up a fight to make miracles happen. Accidents and illness do not just take care of themselves. Even in the gravest situations hope exists if we choose to find it.

14

EVEN DEATH CAN OPEN A DOOR

"Is death the last sleep?
No, it is the last and final awakening."
SIR WALTER SCOTT *(1771–1832),*
Scottish novelist and poet

"Tears hinder sorrow from becoming despair."
J. H. LEIGH HUNT *(1784–1859),*
English author

No one can prepare for tragedy. We do not learn from the sufferings of others, or so it has been said—we must suffer ourselves. In any case, let the stories in the following pages offer hope that unexpected opportunities really do present themselves out of life's most painful experiences.

MAKE RELATIONSHIPS STRONGER.

When a death occurs, don't let the opportunity pass by for improving relationships with friends and family. Life is too precious for fights. Take the initiative to make changes for the better. It may not happen all at once, but keep up your efforts. For Jane Dailey, a free-lance writer and editor, the sudden loss of one parent unexpectedly opened the door to a more meaningful relationship with the other.

When my mother died suddenly of a stroke at age sixty-four, my four sisters and I began to see our father in a new light. My mother had been the parent who always showed affection, smoothed the fights. When she died, Dad let his emotions out. He shared in our grief, offered hugs and support, and sometimes needed them himself. None of us had ever seen him cry before, and he did. My mother's death has brought out a caring side of him that was hidden when she was alive. The distance between us is gone. Our family is closer than ever.

LET THE TRAGEDY OF ANOTHER OPEN THE DOOR TO RECOVERY.

For musician and lyricist Elton John, it was the death of Ryan White, the young boy whose battle with AIDS touched the hearts of millions, that opened the door to recovery after fifteen years of drugs and alcoholism.

In a television interview with David Frost, John spoke of how the White family's ability to show compassion and forgiveness made him realize how out of touch he was with the basics in life, and how much he wished he could be like them. The experience of visiting Ryan White as he was dying, and being personally connected with his courageous family, convinced Elton John that it was time to listen to what those who loved him had told him to do for years—end his addictions. For Elton John that marked the beginning of a new phase of life that would include a profound new appreciation for other people.

CARING CAN START A DOMINO EFFECT.

The friendship between Norman Brickell and Ralph Eckelman, as reported by Douglas Martin in *The New York Times,* is filled with a whole sequence of doors closing and opening in the face of tragedy. As their story illustrates, new doors can open a little at a time, each increment increasing the level of caring and chance for happiness.

The two men met when Mr. Brickell offered to help the wheelchair-bound Mr. Eckelman across a busy city street. Mr. Eckelman turned him down by explaining that he was on his way to Central Park to train for the New York City Marathon. Mr. Brickell, struggling with the suicide of his eighteen-year-old son and a recent divorce, found in Mr. Eckelman a person who would accept his honest caring and assistance in training for the road race. For Mr. Eckelman, a fifty-year-old reformed alcoholic with cerebral palsy, the chance meeting with Mr. Brickell was but one of several opportunities that had changed his situation for the good. Not only had he conquered drinking—"I got sick and tired of getting sick and tired" is how he describes his triumph—but he had also discovered that, unlike his homebound twin brother, he was not mentally retarded; dyslexia was what had been preventing him from understanding how to read. With that discovery he was able to pursue a high school diploma. Through support groups Mr. Eckelman has offered his help to others who need it. Through friendship he has provided Mr. Norman Brickell with a rare chance to make a "personal contribution" in life, after experiencing profound tragedy.

"There are no times in life when opportunity, the chance to be and do, gathers so richly about the soul as when it has to suffer. Then everything depends on whether the man turns to the lower or the higher helps. If he resorts to mere expedients and tricks, the opportunity is lost. He comes out no richer nor greater; nay, he comes out harder, poorer, smaller, for his pain. But if he turns to God, the hour of suffering is the turning hour of his life."
PHILLIPS BROOKS (1835–1893),
American Episcopal bishop

TAKE CONTROL OF TODAY, LET
TOMORROW TAKE CARE OF ITSELF.

Psychiatrist Viktor Frankl, Nazi death camp sur-
vivor and author of *Man's Search for Meaning*,
describes how a young invalid boy, in writing of his
impending death to a friend, recalled a movie in
which the hero awaited death with courage and
dignity. The boy concluded that he'd been given a
similar chance, an opportunity to make an accomplishment out of dying.

In a quote from his letter to *The New York Times*,
an AIDS patient sees his greatest accomplishment as
seizing the chance to live a better life than before:

> *I'm a human being with choices, and I choose not to live
> with this cloud over my head. I believe we can shape our
> own fate. I have to believe that. HIV has been a more
> positive influence in my life than a negative one. I'm a
> more focused, settled person. I have a good, loving rela-
> tionship and I am lucky to have a supportive family.
> Meditation, vitamins, visualization, audiotapes, exer-
> cise, good friends (and maybe even acupuncture, if I ever
> get up the nerve) are all a part of my life now. I keep my
> eyes and ears open for new and not-so-new treatments
> and therapies that may enhance my life and make me a
> healthier and stronger person.*

Other AIDS patients may express powerlessness
over the situation, but he believes he is far from

powerless. "Turn this into a challenge—a challenge to live a long, healthy, productive life," he says to others in his situation. "Go ahead and plan for the future; you just may find yourself experiencing it."

The personal response to death, and the prospect of death, determines whether anything good can come of it—whether a new door will open.

Do not try to rush through the grieving stage.

DO NOT DENY THE EXPRESSION OF ANGER OR GRIEF—OR ANY EMOTION, FOR THAT MATTER.

BUILD A NETWORK OF SUPPORT. EXPAND IN IT.

Talk about your feelings with those who share in your grief, as well as with those who have experienced similar tragedies and found ways to cope.

People react differently to death and tragedy; do not hold it against them if they react in ways you hadn't anticipated or in ways that disappoint you.

When a parent or other loved one in a family dies,

try to step out of established roles and form a closer relationship with those who remain behind.

Be patient with the steps it takes, emotionally and physically, to make a new door open.

CONSIDER EVERY INCH THAT ALLOWS LIGHT INTO A DARK SITUATION A TRIUMPH.

15

PINE'S PEARLS OF WISDOM

This book has focused on one way people find success in life, by turning a negative experience into a positive one.

Through the wise and generous insights of our contributors, each stumble and success described is a powerful testament to hope in difficult times—an attitude that, along with optimism, can be cultivated by anyone. With that objective in mind this chapter presents the guiding principles of hope and optimism as culled from the previous pages. We hope you will use these morsels of wisdom and inspiration, gleaned in hindsight, as your keys for opening that next door to success and happiness.

1. SO A DOOR CLOSES ... SO WHAT?

A firing is not such a bad thing. You will land on your feet again if you have complete confidence in yourself and your abilities.

Being out of work can work to your advantage.

Take that closed door as a sign that fate has other plans for you.

Nothing is impossible.

Unexpected roads are waiting to be traveled. Do not panic when a door closes. Something great will come of it if you don't let it get you down.

2. QUICK TURNAROUNDS

I believe in me—that's what you've got to say to yourself. Stick to your dreams. Do everything you can to realize them. The rest will take care of itself.

You can't succeed every time.

A door could open when you need it the most.

Life is full of surprises. Opportunities come along whether you're ready for them or not. They either happen, or you make them happen.

3. DON'T GIVE UP!

Where there is a will, there is a way. If there is a chance in a million that you can do something, anything, to keep what you want from ending, do it. Pry the door open or, if need be, wedge your foot in that door and keep it open.

Never take no for an answer.

A reversal isn't always the end of the road, it may just be a detour.

Think of changing your role in the game if it keeps you in what you love.

It doesn't matter how many times you fail, all you need is one success.

Persistence pays off.

Don't take a silent response to be a negative response.

Hopelessness is a relative state. If you see a crack, lean on it. Give that door a good hard push; throw your weight against it. Don't give up.

4. <u>NOW WHAT?</u>

Accept the prospect of change. That's the only way you can move ahead.

Be glad when you don't always get your own way.

Everything has a purpose; everything has its own time.

Don't dwell on what could have been done differently. That's another way of resisting change, and it can only keep you down.

Even if the door's closing was your fault, don't keep on blaming yourself for it. Take positive action. Make the changes necessary so that what happened once doesn't happen again.

5. TAKE TIME OUT—TO THINK!

Don't always blame the other fellow.

Turn a situation over and over in your mind until that new idea emerges. Find ways to get your thinking out of a rut and new ideas will come.

Yes, you can do anything you want to do.

Try, stop, and think. Then try again. Find a better way in.

Humor cushions the blow. Learn to laugh at yourself and your circumstances.

Keep an upbeat attitude as you struggle through.

6. <u>KEEP MOVING!</u>

Take action! You can't let rejection keep you down.

Your biggest break can come from never quitting. Being at the right place at the right time can only happen when you keep moving toward the next opportunity.

An unhappy situation may be your back door to success.

Use the feeling of defeat as your motivation to get out of a bad situation.

Don't let defeat flatten you.

Use a bad situation to overcome other obstacles in your life. Treat tough times like gym equipment. Use them to make you tougher.

Give yourself a second chance.

7. TELL YOUR STORY

Share your situation with someone who values your talent. Don't run away and hide. *It's all right to ask for help when doors close.*

Show 'em you can do it!

Bad news? Share it! You'd be surprised at how people can help if you just let them know your situation.

Get the word out.

Keep up your friendships; keep up your contacts. Reach out to others. It's all right to ask for help. People are more willing to help than you might think.

8. GET MAD!

Am I ever going to show them they made a mistake! When a door closes, use constructive anger as a positive force to open new doors.

Let "healthy hurt" keep you going. Don't look for scapegoats or place blame, but express your anger as a way to rid your system of toxic feelings.

9. TRY ANYTHING!

It's never too late to move ahead. Go in with an open mind and find out for yourself whether a new opportunity exists.

Give yourself room for letting something better come of a bad situation.

Believe in your abilities. Try something new and different and you will make it.

Don't let ego stand in your way. Keep an open mind when it comes to putting a value on your services.

Listen to others, but make up your own mind. In the end, let your own final judgment be the determining factor as to whether an opportunity exists.

What have you got to lose?

Don't let a negative attitude be an obstacle.

There's nothing wrong with a little ignorance.

10. SEIZE SERENDIPITY

Keep your eyes open for serendipity. Be prepared to recognize when you are at the right place at the right time—and to act.

Don't let the right time pass you by.

Put yourself in the vicinity of your dreams.

11. BUILD A DOOR

There are no guarantees in life. Sometimes you must be willing to take a chance.

Use the closed door as your inspiration to accomplish more than you ever thought you could. Don't wait for a death sentence to explode into action. Your future becomes what you make it.

Work, work, work—but always with a winning attitude.

When you step out and take a chance, chances are you are ready for a big success. Do not let the fear of failure turn you back or wait too long to make a move.

Don't just dream about the possibilities for making a new start. Plan your exit.

12. YOUR TURN TO CLOSE A DOOR?

Put yourself first. Do not be afraid to close a door on someone else. Use your self-respect as a source of courage to speak out and close a door.

Step in, speak up, and be ready to close the door. Find out what's going on. Discuss it. Risk dire consequences. The truth will provide peace of mind.

13. MIRACLES OUT OF MISHAPS

The darkest moments can turn out to the good.

The good seldom comes by mistake. Treat recovery time as a rare chance for introspection and self-discovery.

Fate is what you make of it.

Serious accidents increase one's appreciation for the suffering of others.

Let others hear from you in their time of suffering. Put up a fight to make miracles happen. In hopeless situations hope exists if we choose to find it.

14. EVEN DEATH CAN OPEN A DOOR

Let death give you the opportunity to make relationships stronger.

Mark tragedy with something meaningful. Turn your love for the deceased into a living memorial that will help others.

Let the tragedy of another open the door to recovery.

Caring can start a domino effect.

Take control of today, let tomorrow take care of itself.

Do not deny the expression of anger or grief—or any emotion, for that matter.

Build a network of support. Expand on it.

Consider every inch that allows light into a dark situation a triumph.